Great Liberty

FRONTISPIECE BY ANDRÉ MASSON

Great Liberty

JULIEN GRACQ

TRANSLATED BY GEORGE MACLENNAN

WAKEFIELD PRESS

CAMBRIDGE, MASSACHUSETTS

Wakefield Press, P.O. Box 425645, Cambridge, MA 02142

Originally published in 1946 as *Liberté grande* © ÉDITIONS CORTI, 1961.
Frontispiece by André Masson from the French edition
© 2023 Artists Rights Society (ARS), New York / ADAGP, Paris

This book was set in Garamond Premier Pro and Helvetica Neue Pro by Wakefield Press. Printed and bound by Sheridan Saline, Inc., in the United States of America.

ISBN: 978-1-939663-89-4

Available through D.A.P./Distributed Art Publishers
75 Sixth Avenue, Suite 630
New York, New York 10004
Tel: (212) 627-1999
Fax: (212) 627-9484

10 9 8 7 6 5 4 3 2 1

CONTENTS

TRANSLATOR'S INTRODUCTION

Julien Gracq is recognized in France as a major novelist and writer; he's one of the few who lived to see his collected works enshrined in a Bibliothèque de la Pléiade edition, thus assuring their canonical status. Outside France he enjoys a high reputation among connoisseurs of continental literature but only a low profile among the book-buying public. Gracq would have shrugged his shoulders at that, but by any measure he is a writer of stature, a sovereign stylist with a distinctive imaginative vision.

Born Louis Poirier in Saint-Florent-Le-Vieil in the Loire Valley in 1910, he studied geography and, though a high-achieving student, pursued a modest career as a schoolteacher, retaining his birth name for all save literary purposes. After 1970 he enjoyed a lengthy retirement, reaching the grand age of ninety-seven, still writing but publishing no more fiction.

Marginality suited Gracq. He was forthright in disapproving of key postwar French cultural trends, notably existentialism and the Nouveau Roman; in a polemical essay of 1950 he condemned what he saw as a complacent and compromised French literary establishment.[1] He is well known for having refused the Prix Goncourt for his 1951 novel *Le Rivage des Syrtes* (*The Opposing Shore*).

Although his main claim to fame is as a novelist, his output of fiction over a lengthy writing career was small. In his lifetime, he wrote four novels and two novellas; an unfinished novel has been published subsequent to his death. He wrote, however, an equal quantity of nonfiction, some of it making its way into English thanks to Ingeborg Kohn's translations. An overview of his œuvre suggests that an emphasis on the novels, though understandable, does something of a disservice to the balance he maintained between different forms of writing—dramatic, polemical, critical, essayistic, topographical, autobiographical, and, not least, poetic.

Although not himself a surrealist, Gracq was in profound sympathy with the movement and maintained friendly relations with André Breton and a number of surrealist artists and writers. In 1947, he published *André Breton*, an extended study that argued for Breton's distinctive qualities as a writer. Appreciation went in both directions; in 1939, Breton had written to Gracq, expressing a strongly felt response to his first novel, *Au Château d'Argol* (*The Castle of Argol*). In a talk given a few years later, Breton declared that surrealism had reached its high watermark "on the literary level" with this work.

Breton's admiration is surprising in one respect: though a work of rare oneiric intensity, *Au Château d'Argol* is lacking in any element of oneiric irrationality. "It is," Gracq said of surrealism, "the language, the sense of the sentence, the eloquence, the poetry that seduced me, rather than the content."[2] Gracq's fiction, written for the most part in a burnished prose style, conveys the atmo-spheres and attitudes of reverie rather than *rêve*.[3] His protagonists are caught up in intimate dramas involving doubt, dilemma, and interior reflection. Keats's notion of negative capability is a good fit for his fiction: when one is "capable of being in uncertainties, mysteries, doubts, without any irritable reaching after fact and reason." While his stories house no ghosts, they are peopled by haunted characters and located in sites conducive to haunting.[4] "It's toward borders, frontiers that the action of my novels is situ-ated";[5] settings such as Argol (specifically indebted to Udolpho and the House of Usher) are threshold environments shaded by a prevailing sense of mystery.[6] Gracq's 1958 novel *Un Balcon en forêt* (*A Balcony in the Forest*) comes closer to the conventions of realism; nevertheless, its forest setting maintains his emphasis on liminality: the Ardennes of 1939 merges with "la forêt galante de Shakespeare"[7]—Shakespeare's forest of Arden.

Gracq's limited output of fiction came to a near halt after the publication of *A Balcony in the Forest*. Much of the second volume of the Pléiade *Oeuvres complètes* is taken up by nonfiction—a variety of essayistic, autobiographical, and personal writings, reflections on literature and the arts, and topographical explora-tions. Between 1953 and 1956 he worked on a novel, *Les terres du couchant* (The sunset lands), but was unable to resolve a conclu-sion and so abandoned it. Published posthumously in 2014, it is, although unconcluded, a substantial and accomplished work that easily stands shoulder to shoulder with the four finished novels.

One of the least-known strands of Gracq's oeuvre is his explicitly poetic writing. The present translation aims to present a version of his solitary volume of prose poems, *Liberté grande*—*Great Liberty*.

This, his most avant-garde work, stands, as Bernhild Boie notes, in marked contrast with his fiction:

> When Julien Gracq talks of poetic creation it's almost always as opposed to the writing of fiction. Narration requires a certain solidity and bows to a certain number of constraints. . . . The poem, on the other hand, emerges in a single outpouring . . . , a miraculous fluidity of words and images, as the title *Great Liberty* loudly proclaims.[8]

Here Gracq, for once, gives full rein to surrealist delirium. For this alone, *Great Liberty* would be noteworthy, but I would argue further that his prose poems, more so than his fiction, touch on Gracq's deepest concerns and provide a vehicle for expressing his creative vision.

In 1930, as a young student, Gracq discovered surrealism by way of Breton's *Nadja* and Max Ernst's visual collage novel, *La Femme 100 têtes*. The encounter was revelatory: "An entire *terra incognita* of sensibility suddenly opened up for me with these two books and I know of no other writing that gave me such a feeling of annexation, that of a vast territory explored and at the same time assimilated forever."[9] Alone among Gracq's writings, *Great Liberty* utilizes techniques learned from Breton and Ernst to explore that *terra incognita*. Gracq scholar Bernhild Boie puts the matter succinctly: "The first collection's prose draws inspiration from the surrealist experiment in automatic writing."[10] For a further understanding of

Gracq's foray into avant-garde poetry, we must consider the circumstances under which he wrote these texts.

With the outbreak of war in 1939, Gracq—as Louis Poirier—was mobilized as an infantry lieutenant and led his troop on various patrols in Holland, Belgium, and the Nord de France. Following an experience of combat, he was captured near Dunkirk in June 1940 and held as a prisoner of war in the Hoyerswerda camp in Silesia. A lung infection led to his release in February 1941. Over the next eighteen months he took up a succession of teaching posts and started writing again. He had, in Hoyerswerda, conceived a second novel, *Un Beau ténébreux* (*A Dark Stranger*), and had written its prologue.[11] Following his release, however, he put the project on hold and wrote instead two accounts of his wartime experiences, one a directly autobiographical testament, *Souvenirs de guerre*, and the other a transposition into fiction of the climactic events of the memoir, a novella simply titled *Récit*. These remained in manuscript form, and it was only after his death that they were jointly published, as *Manuscrits de guerre*.[12] At the same time, however, Gracq was exploring a radically different form of writing. Between 1941 and 1942 he accumulated a group of forty hallucinatory and surrealistic prose poems, primarily (though not exclusively) experimenting with automatic writing. Some of these then appeared in various journals, with the entire corpus finally published in 1946. Much of the discussion that follows in this introduction will focus on the texts contained in the 1946 edition; the texts added to the expanded later editions are best addressed separately.

André Breton, who as a medical student had studied psychology, tells how, with Philippe Soupault in 1919, he undertook to explore the phenomenon of "psychic automatism":[13]

> I resolved to obtain from myself what one seeks to obtain from a patient—a spoken monologue uttered as rapidly as possible, over which the critical faculty of the subject has no control. . . . It was with this in mind that Philippe Soupault . . . and I undertook to cover some paper with writing, with a laudable contempt for what might result in terms of literature.[14]

With this act surrealism came into being. The psychiatric background is worth bearing in mind; V. H. Martinez, while noting the potential psychological dangers of automatic writing, adds that, in moderation, the practice could also be therapeutic: "Throughout his life, Breton sometimes wrote automatically, predominantly in periods of spiritual crisis. . . . Automatic writing, cultivated with moderation, could also help to transcend a harming or a traumatic phase."[15] As Bernhild Boie's studies of Gracq's manuscripts have shown, it's a moderated practice of automatic writing that accounts for many of the *Great Liberty* texts of the early 1940s:

> Surrender and control are often divided into two distinct movements of writing. In a first phase, the poem seems to build itself freely without immediate scrutiny. Immediate corrections are rare, the connections fall into place spontaneously. The will to control, to correct, to revisit only appears subsequently. Marginal additions, retouchings, deletions, bear witness to a rigorous and careful work of revision.

There is indeed a certain idea of form here that influences the course of the writing.[16]

Might such a modified form of automatic writing have been thera-peutic for Gracq? We can't know the answer to this, but in a broad-er sense Boie confirms that it enabled release and even euphoria: "Questioned later on the attraction that this new genre held for him, Julien Gracq will explain it in terms of immediate, dazzling plea-sure. The work of poetry offers itself to him as creative play."[17]

Gracq's experiences of 1940–1941 were nothing if not trau-matic. The disheartening impact of hapless, seemingly pointless military maneuvers is evident from the *Souvenirs de guerre*: "one of the foulest moments of my life," he said of the abject May 1940 retreat before the German onslaught.[18] There followed, in rapid succession, capture, imprisonment, and illness. If Gracq left the *Manuscrits de guerre* unpublished, one suspects that it wasn't only on account of discretion (the texts focus unblinkingly on a mo-ment of national disgrace), but because, if only by force of cir-cumstance, their narratives approach too closely the condition of absurdity and angst that he rejected in Sartre and Camus. The poems, as "creative play," moved in exactly the opposite direction. Gracq began work on them after he was released not only from Hoyerswerda, but, no less importantly, from a military rank and responsibility that he had come to detest. Here, in the most literal sense, was a great liberation: the volume's title is celebratory on more than one count. The poem-texts seem to have exploded from his pen in a manner without parallel in his creative career, and it's reasonable to suppose that he derived benefit from writing them.

It's likely that with the 1946 version of *Great Liberty* Gracq intended to bypass the pressure of wartime concerns, and so he does, but not entirely. "Cortège" is the most fragmentary of the *Liberty* texts, and one of the most elusive:

> Men 40–horses 8, this single regulatory inscription announced the mortuary bogie from afar—in waiting for more expressive marks of the glorious resurrection—not without having paraded in good order—only momentarily slowed by ascending the ramp—the first-class saloon cars where jade jewels sparkled on the fingers of pretty bridge players—busy passing the time that only materialized from one moment to the next—the one that the *dead man* wanted to devote to finally putting his cards on the table—the glance thrown through the car door on the moving and rainy expanse of an indifferent landscape.

Boie explains the phrase "Men 40–horses 8": "Until the end of the Second World War, this inscription, placed on wagons of timber goods (to indicate capacity in case of mobilization), didn't fail to strike observers as seeming to establish an equivalence with transports destined for the front lines."[19] What is the destination of the funeral wagon bearing the living dead? The front lines? Somewhere even darker? The Vichy roundup of French Jews was in full swing through the spring and summer of 1942. If he was writing at this time,[20] Gracq would certainly have been aware of the notorious July roundup in Paris that saw 13,000 men, women, and children interned and then sent on to the death camps. Reading the poem in this light can only be a matter of conjecture, but the text is resonant with ominous implications.

It was some years before Gracq felt able to address the events of the Second World War openly as an imaginative writer. Published in 1958, *A Balcony in the Forest* is set during the "faux guerre" of 1939–1940. Lieutenant Grange's experiences in the novel are alleviated by a posting to the timeless, sheltering presence of the Ardennes Forest, where he is able to enjoy a prolonged respite from the looming German threat. This contrasts with the earlier, fact-based *Récit*, where the portrayal of Lieutenant G's war is unremittingly fraught and sometimes palpably angry. The year 1958 also saw the second edition of *Great Liberty*, augmented by an additional eight texts, one of which, "Gomorrah," evokes a later episode of Gracq's war. The text, Boie tells us, relates the writer's journey out of Caen at the end of May 1944. "Gomorrah, the city destroyed by fire descending from heaven, refers to the fate of Caen in 1944."[21] Caen, where Gracq had held a temporary university post, was devastated by Allied bombing during the Battle of Normandy; Gracq's timely exit was a narrow escape. However, title aside, little of this grimness is apparent in the text. There are tanks lying in wait in the woods and images of aerial combat, but the tone throughout is relaxed, nonchalant. By 1958 Gracq's experiences of war had acquired an imaginative life of their own and so were able to supersede his sense in 1941–1942 of a miserably lived experience.[22]

Returning to the 1946 *Great Liberty*, there are, besides "Cortège," vanishingly few traces of the war, and nothing comparable to "Gomorrah." But the absence of direct reference conceals some uneasy undercurrents. One notes the casual allusions to Berezina and Waterloo, surreptitious reminders of the retreat and defeat of Napoleon's *Grande Armée*.[23] The volume's inaugural text, "To Galvanize Urbanism," is densely seeded with cultural references—Rimbaud, De Quincey, Baudelaire, *L'Âge d'or*, Wagner's *Flying Dutchman*, de Chirico, Lesage's *Le Diable boiteux*, Greek mythology, and the Bible. One further reference sits oddly in this elite company: "Through the window of the railway carriage, one also dreams, caught in the lens of a periscope, of the landing site of Wells's giant tripods from Mars." On an imaginary or remembered journey, the writer's train is approaching the Breton port city of Saint-Nazaire, where he looks out at "thickets of giant cranes with horizontal arms," a view that, we presume, evokes for him the image of the Martian war machines of *The War of the Worlds*. A reference to a story about invasion by a technologically superior alien force was far from innocuous at this time, when Saint-Nazaire was occupied by German forces busy building a formidable submarine base.[24] *A Balcony in the Forest* will subsequently confirm this subtext; nocturnal military searchlights remind Lieutenant Grange of Wells's "giant unwell Martians."[25]

From the vantage point of its posthumous publication, we can also detect a few links between the *Manuscrits de guerre* and *Great Liberty*. The otherwise matter-of-fact war memoir indulges in a brief burst of rhetoric: "Rimbaldian railway stations in the sonorous night."[26] The allusion reminds us that, in 1870, the teenage Rimbaud was on the front line of the Franco-Prussian war where he witnessed the Prussian shelling of Charleville. The importance of Rimbaud as a precedent for *Great Liberty* is evident from the volume's epigraph, a quotation from *Illuminations*, but the "Rimbaldian railway stations" further indicate an awareness of Rimbaud's historical moment, which, to a limited but significant degree, was analogous with Gracq's. The former's poem of carefree wartime vagabondage, "Au Cabaret Vert," may well have influenced Gracq's "Gomorrah"—another oddly idyllic evocation of wartime vagabondage.[27]

★

"To Galvanize Urbanism" concludes on an anarchistic note: the devil "will never be finished with blowing up roofs." In Lesage's eighteenth-century satirical fantasy *Le Diable boiteux* (The lame devil), the demon Asmodeus is able to supernaturally lift the roofs off Madrid houses. Gracq's devil is more destructive, and the context of 1941 prompts the thought of aerial bombing. One of the poem-texts, "Landscape," perversely proposes a bomb blast as a liberatory phenomenon: "Suddenly, it was also all the music of bombings, when the airy landscape, eased by a breath, allows a minute's playful relaxation of the laws of gravity." This repeats and adapts a sentence in Gracq's contemporaneous war story, *Récit*: "The whole world was like a house breathed on by a bomb, allowing a second's spirited play with the laws of gravity."[28] The "scandalous" character of the image—written in time of war—is consonant with its surrealism; in *André Breton* (1947) we read that: "The surrealists revered [poetry] for its unequalled coefficient of expansion; in the mineshafts that they sought to excavate in every direction so as to escape from their jail, it played for them the role of the most *shattering* of explosives."[29] Gracq too wished to escape from a metaphorical jail. "To Galvanize Urbanism" cites the myth of Amphion, who built the walls of Thebes by means of the music created by his voice and his lyre: "It's to this myth, in which the interrogation of the most overwhelming constraints of heaviness is so lucidly made to rely on the purest breath of the spirit, that I would like to confide the secret hopes that I continue to nourish of not being the eternal prisoner of this squalid street of shops." These hopes might be realized not so much by Amphion's lyre as by the surrealist poetics that the writer chose to embrace—a supply of dynamite for a liberatory explosion.

Hart Crane commented on the "rapturous and explosive destructivism of Rimbaud,"[30] while, in her study of Rimbaud in the context of the Paris Commune, Kristin Ross paraphrases a comment of Sartre's: "[Rimbaud's] metaphor explodes and scatters in all directions."[31] The metaphor is literalized in Gracq when, in "Surprise Party at the House of the Augustules," books explode in secondhand bookstalls. Explosive imagery recurs as a metaphor in *A Balcony in the Forest* where, at a pregnant moment for Lieutenant Grange, there's an explosion of possibility—"la *possibilité* explose."[32] In *Au Chateau d'Argol*, at another critical moment, it's "as though every phenomenon was then taken to its ultimate power of *explosion*."[33]

An account by Terry Eagleton of Rimbaud's prose poetry might be extended to the texts of *Great Liberty*: "The prose poem is straggling, indeterminately bounded, equivalencing, paratactic, replete with a density and dizziness that mark the point where language is about to take off beyond language."[34] And, one might add, where language is taken to its ultimate power of explosion. Most obviously, the sentence as a closed unit is exploded in a number of the 1946 texts. The surrealist bomb blast allows a suspension, a relaxation, and sometimes a disordering of syntactic rules:[35]

For that natural and anarchical society of words, able to proliferate spontaneously by itself (this is shown by automatic writing), syntax, on the contrary, represents an order and a hierarchy irremediably imposed from the outside by means of a brutal, rational conquest. Subjected to the rational yoke of syntax, in order to *serve* . . . , the word nonetheless remains in rebellion against all definitive subjection.[36]

Gracq's image of revolt against an imposed hierarchy is occasioned by André Breton's writings, but they also return us to Rimbaud's prose poetry and its proximity, as argued by Kristen Ross, to the Paris Commune. The 1946 *Great Liberty*, for its part, aims in good measure to disrupt a syntactic apparatus of "order and hierarchy" in favor of Rimbaud's *alchimie du verbe*. If readers are prepared to accept the *Great Liberty* texts as instances of creative anarchy in action, then their reward is the delirious fascination and imaginative freedom of surrealist poetry in full flight.

It's further worth noting that Gracq's exploration of Breton's language in the 1947 study doubles, in effect, as an extended discussion of his own poetic practice,[37] thus providing a key to the creative and linguistic prerogatives of *Great Liberty*. For most readers of Gracq, *Great Liberty* is a marginal work, one that's little known to his Anglophone readers. From the perspective of *André Breton*, however, it emerges as a work that, for Gracq himself, was far from marginal. The fact that he continued to add to it over a number of years should by itself testify to its importance for him.

In "Truro," "space is strangely measured by rooms that are prey to an abnormal thickening of the walls." The buildup of dead matter is a contaminant that gives rise to fears of subjective reification, for "such rooms are the dwelling place not only of the body, but also the imagination." Here, again, is the proximity of a threat that Gracq, no doubt in the wake of Hoyerswerda, seems to have felt keenly; he accuses Malraux and the existentialists of indulging in "the problem of the prison. . . . How to live in prison."[38] By contrast, *Great Liberty* is, as the title implies, anticarceral: it sets a value instead on buoyancy, lightness, and mobility, qualities associated with speed, freedom of movement, metamorphic fluidity, and creative agency.

"To Galvanize Urbanism," the opening text of *Great Liberty*, is a remarkable document, one that stakes out a distinct discursive field, a composite of surrealist poetry, personal essay, and fantastic urbanist manifesto. But, at the same time, its clotted prose is a less than ideal medium for attaining creative freedom and seems to have been a path that Gracq chose not to follow much further. If surrealist dislocations—taking this word in its root sense—offer Gracq the cutting edge of the tool—a free-running pen—that might allow him to slice through the bloated and imprisoning mass of the metropolis ("that belly flab") and so realize a musical dream of mobility and liberty, then this must be fulfilled as *re*location: "Luxury is, above all, a marvelously green horizon dilated with nearby music, face upturned to a sky as green as the meadows, the delicious wind of costly speed spread evenly over the face" ("Grand Hotel").

In "To Galvanize Urbanism," Gracq quotes a phrase from Rimbaud: "to Circeto of the icy heights." He chooses, so he tells us, to understand the word "Circeto" as a place name. This "erroneous" reading (it should be a woman's name) is in line with the place names that proliferate throughout *Great Liberty* and sparks the elated and kaleidoscopic spatial fantasia of the text's middle section:

> . . . like the celestial visitation of eternal snows in the light of day, their touch on each summit of glory in a Pentecostal light—the eye raised from under an impossible angle perceives in a nocturnal winter sky lighthouse beacons revolving amidst sarabands of snow, long, splendid vehicles slipping noiselessly along swept avenues . . .

The poet's free imagination, speeding across visionary panoramic vistas, eventually returns to the spectacle of the city, but a very different one from Paris, namely Saint-Nazaire, the "one real city that moves me to rapture." Saint-Nazaire is seen as "a city ocean-bound from everywhere"—afloat on the waters. It can hardly be a coincidence that *Great Liberty*'s immediately succeeding text is "Venice," a city that is literally afloat. From this point on, the often strenuous and congested prose that characterizes "To Galvanize Urbanism" is much less in evidence. The subsequent first edition texts are shorter, and their flowingly impressionistic style allows greater latitude for both imaginative free play and a phantasmatic expansion of possibilities. Bernhild Boie evokes "a passing moment, a magical instant, . . . the minute when matter is divested of its weight, when the tree dreams of flight, and when a man dreams of rejoining the immateriality of his mirror image."[39] Such moments correspond to Gracq's deepest understanding of surrealism; the talismanic word that recurs throughout *André Breton* is "liberation."

However, while liberation is a central concern of *Great Liberty*, it's accompanied by other less rhapsodic ingredients, for example whimsicality, weirdness, and a sometimes jarring dissonance resulting from collaged juxtapositions:[40]

> The evenings bordered with eglantines, the fine mornings of trout fishing documentaries that stir whole fistfuls of gems in a salad bowl ("Gang").

> The assembly line worker, skilled at reckoning the soft flow of the minutes with his index finger, suddenly imagines a particular remission of his dream and falls asleep. The connecting rods and drive belts are suddenly sprinkled with primroses. The world dozes, scarcely time enough to sneeze an *Ave Maria* ("Society Scandals").

Such bizarre image-formations can be referred back to Rimbaud's statement in *A Season in Hell*: "I explained my magical sophistry with the hallucination of words."[41]

The texts added to the subsequent 1958 and 1966 editions of *Great Liberty* are contained in a separate, concluding section bearing the ecological title *La Terre habitable* (The habitable earth). There is further surrealist prose here, but this later section also brings a qualitative shift in tone; as it traverses given geographical territories—the Andes, the Flemish polders, the countryside of Normandy, the Massif Central—Gracq's poetic writing is increasingly bound to a felt earth. The geographical and topographical dimension of *Great Liberty* will be further addressed in the afterword, by way of a discussion of "The Siesta in Dutch Flanders," a text that has been described by the Belgian writer Jacques de Decker, with perhaps just a touch of partiality, as "that fascinating prose, one of the most beautiful in the French language."[42] Certainly, nothing else Gracq wrote so movingly and effectively expresses his deep imaginative engagement with a "habitable earth."

★

Acknowledgments are due to Bernhild Boie. Her authoritative commentary and notes in the Pléiade *Oeuvres complètes* were an invaluable resource on which I've drawn freely. I'm indebted to Clive Scott and Marie-Noelle Guillot for taking the time to advise me on the points I queried, clarifying some issues and correcting and improving a few of my readings. Finally, I'm grateful to Marc Lowenthal of Wakefield Press for supporting this project, also, along with Judy Feldmann, for valuable editorial input.

NOTES

All references to Gracq's writings, with the exception of the *Manuscrits de guerre*, are taken from the two volumes of his *Oeuvres complètes*, vol. 1, edited by Bernhild Boie; vol. 2, edited by Bernhild Boie and Claude Dourguin (Paris: Gallimard, Bibliothèque de la Pléiade, 1989 and 1995, respectively). These are referenced in the notes below as *OC* 1 and *OC* 2. Translations from these sources are my own. The translation of *Great Liberty* is based on the 2006 José Corti edition but cross-checked against the Pléiade text as established by Bernhild Boie.

1. "La Littérature à l'estomac" (The literature of the stomach), in *OC* 1.

2. *OC* 2, 1034.

3. Commenting on *André Breton*, Boie points out that Gracq promotes Henri Bergson at the expense of Sigmund Freud, something that serves "to surreptitiously slide from the notion of *rêve*, so important to the surrealists, to that of *reverie*, which is what matters for Gracq" (*OC* 1, 1283).

4. Commenting on gothic fiction in a 1965 interview, Gracq remarked: "Above all I love the accessories put into play in these novels: ruined castles, ghosts, nocturnal noises—I've often dreamed of a book in which they would feature less naively" (*OC* 1, 1130).

5. *OC* 2, 1204.

6. Gracq acknowledged his debt to *The Mysteries of Udolpho* and *The Fall of the House of Usher* in the "Avis au lecteur" which prefaces *Argol*. This is omitted from Louise Varese's English translation.

7. *OC* 2, 123.

8. Bernhild Boie, "Julien Gracq, *Liberté grande*, présenté par Bernhild Boie," (*Genesis (Manuscrits-Recherche-Invention)* 17 (2001): 151–179, https://www.persee.fr/doc/item_1167-5101_2001_num_17_1_1203).

9. *OC* 2, 1034.

10. Boie, "Julien Gracq, *Liberté grande*, présenté par Bernhild Boie."

11. The novel was not, as is sometimes said, written while Gracq was interned in Hoyerswerda. Christopher Moncrieff's afterword to his translation of *A Dark Stranger* (London: Pushkin Press, 2013) is responsible for this canard: "In *Carnets du grand chemin* [Gracq] describes how he wrote it in bed in the prison hut." A more careful reading of the *Carnets* passage indicates that Gracq is referring here not to the novel but to the few pages of its prologue. "I would have lacked the strength to undertake it straightaway; however, in order to confirm the decision taken, I wrote

the prologue" (*OC* 2, 1037). Conditions in the camp, the limited period of time spent there, his physical weakness and eventual illness all made the writing of an entire novel inconceivable, above all a subtly meditative drama dense with literary and cultural references. "It's only in the summer of 1942 that Gracq would start work on his second novel" (Boie in *OC* 1, 1209)—he completed it in 1944. In an ironic tribute to the site of its origin, the novel includes a brief reminiscence of the landscape of Hoyerswerda.

12. *Manuscrits de guerre* (Paris: José Corti, 2011), with a foreword by Bernhild Boie. The manuscripts of the *Souvenirs* and the *Récit* are undated, but on available evidence, Boie dates the writing as extending from October 1941 to July 1942.

13. "He [Philippe Soupault] shared Breton's interest in . . . the discoveries outlined by Pierre Janet in his *L'Automatisme psychologique* (the term 'automatic writing,' moreover, was most likely suggested to Breton and Soupault by their reading of Janet, although Breton seems to have taken little else from the renowned psychiatrist)" Mark Polizzotti, *Revolution of the Mind: The Life of André Breton* (London: Bloomsbury, 1995), 105.

14. "The First Surrealist Manifesto," trans. Patrick Waldberg in *Surrealism*, ed. Patrick Waldberg (London: Thames and Hudson, 1972), 71–72.

15. V. H. Martínez, "A Contemporary Scientific Study of André Breton's Automatic Writing," *Barcelona, Research, Art, Creation* 9, no. 2 (2021): 161–184, http://dx.doi.org/10.17583/brac.2021.6341 Martinez.

16. Boie, in *OC* 1, 1212.

17. Boie, in *OC* 1, 1210.

18. *Manuscrits de guerre*, 118.

19. Boie, in *OC* 1, 1234.

20. Bernhild Boie quotes Gracq: "If I range my books on a shelf, I'm uneasy if they aren't in chronological order" (*OC* I, 1223). Following the same principle, "Cortège," coming late in the 1946 sequence, can reasonably be seen as one of the later texts.

21. Boie, in *OC* I, 1238.

22. Cf. Boie: "For a lived experience to become a subject of writing [for Gracq], a temporal distance must first be established. It's as though a theme must get lost in the meanderings of memory (and ripen there) in order to re-emerge in the state of poetic material" (*OC* I, 1288).

23. "A Berezina of fine glass debris" ("The *Bonne Auberge*"); "a Waterloo of the spaces of solitude" ("The Ross Barrier"). Berezina "has entered the French language as a synonym for disaster" (https://www.napoleon.org/en/history-of-the-two-empires/paintings/the-french-army-crossing-the-berezina-on-28-november-1812/). Cf. Gracq's account in the *Souvenirs de guerre* of the French "catastrophe" of 1940—"that troop saturated with defeat like a sponge with water" (*Manuscrits de guerre*, 114).

24. Boie adds a pertinent note to the Saint-Nazaire passage: "This was written at the moment when the Royal Air Force launched its first attacks against the German submarine base in the military port; the bombings will progressively ruin Saint-Nazaire. And it's the simple thought of its destruction now being possible that causes Saint-Nazaire to tip from the universe of real cities into that of imaginary cities" (*OC* I, 1226).

25. *OC* 2, 58.

26. *Manuscrits de guerre*, 43.

27. Eight days I tramped, wearing my boots in holes
    On flinty roads. I came to Charleroi where
    At the Cabaret-Vert I ordered buttered rolls

And fresh-cooked ham not cold yet . . .
        Rimbaud, trans. Brian Hill

28. *Manuscrits de guerre*, 192.

29. *OC* 1, 467.

30. Cited by Henri Peyre in his foreword to Rimbaud, *A Season in Hell; The Illuminations*, translated by Enid Rhodes Peschel (Oxford: Oxford University Press, 1979), vii.

31. "Kristin Ross, *The Emergence of Social Space: Rimbaud and the Paris Commune*, foreword by Terry Eagleton (Hampshire: Macmillan, 1988), 126.

32. *OC* 2, 77.

33. *OC* 1, 23.

34. Eagleton, foreword to Ross, *The Emergence of Social Space*, xi.

35. Gracq's subversion of syntactic clarity and hierarchy, it should be said, is still more radical in the French. This translation scrupulously maintains sentence length and complexity, but I've mediated potential confusion by transposing some clauses and sometimes introducing further punctuation. English prepositions also require more precision than the French *de* and *à*, which can take on more than one prepositional meaning. This flexibility enables Gracq to sometimes loosen and ambiguate his syntax to a degree that is unavailable in English.

36. *André Breton*, *OC* 1, 480–481.

37. "Everything that Gracq takes as essential in Breton's writing is equally valid for his own poetic project" (Boie, in *OC* 1, 1286).

38. *OC* I, 470.

39. Boie, in *OC* I, 1217.

40. Boie comments on Gracq's use of collage in *Great Liberty*: "In the texts 'To Galvanize Urbanism,' 'Furnished Salon,' and 'The Originally Synthetic Unity of Apperception' . . . Gracq makes use of collage or montage to freely exploit surrealist imagery, stage provoking encounters, engender paradoxical spaces, create meaning (or absurdity) through the random use of the most banal words and phrases" (*OC* I, 1214).

41. In "Deliriums II: The Alchemy of the Word," in *A Season in Hell; The Illuminations*, 81.

42. De Decker, "Suzanne Lilar et Julien Gracq: Une amitié littéraire" (Brussels, Royal Academy of French Language and Literature of Belgium, 2008), 6, https://www.arllfb.be/ebibliotheque/communications/dedecker131208.pdf.

Great Liberty

"I'm a transient and not unduly discontented citizen of a metropolis thought to be modern because every known taste has been avoided in the furnishings and the exteriors of houses no less than in the plan of the city. No trace to be found here of any monument to superstition."

Rimbaud, *Illuminations*

TO GALVANIZE URBANISM

Troubled as I always am on the outskirts of a city, but one where, for example, the sight of the pretty couch grass of the Steppes nestling at the foot of the extravagantly priapic skyscrapers would be so enticing, I have, disillusioned with the degrading rot, the interstitial slime of the suburbs and their cancerous aureoles on the maps, lately dreamed of a City laid open with the tool, sliced through and bleeding a living blood, so to speak, of black asphalt from all its severed arteries onto the lushest, most abandoned, most secretive of woodland landscapes. What might we not hope from a city, particularly a feminine one, that, on the altar of a solitary aesthetic concern, agreed to sacrifice that belly flab, not so much bloated as gangrenous, in which, as with childhood chubbiness, the ripest and most glorious beauty, the face of a great city, having been exhausted by the centuries, is perversely ensnared. The butterfly emerging from its cocoon glowing with the colors of dream for, I allow, the shortest, the most doomed of lives, would hardly convey the notion of that fantastic vision of the ship of Paris ready to cast off for a journey to the very bottom of dream, shaking off with the vermin of its hull the inevitable *remora*, the cables and the rotting stays of Economic Servitude. Yes, even forgetting the auditorium where *L'Âge d'or* was shown, it might, following some performance of *Der Fliegende Holländer*, be particularly satisfying to place a distracted foot on the front steps of the Opéra and just once, scarcely surprised by the caress of cool grass, to listen from behind the marine storms of the theater to the penetrating bell of a *real* cow and, coming from between pillars, suddenly shrinking *ad infinitum* as though from a stage effect, be only vaguely amazed by a rustic stampede of frenzied steeds on a *meadow-green* ocean realer than nature.

Am I alone in this? I now dream of this panoramic taste for contrast, a choice of urban blight on the site where the most superfluous constructions will be erected, those most surrendered to luxury, grand hotels for skiers, caravansaries, desert dances, Saharas, the peaks of glaciers, where we find a naïve admission of I don't know what modern need for irony and the life of the hermit. Above all, the words of a Rimbaud poem, which no doubt I've interpreted wrongly—in my own particular way—come back to haunt me: "This evening, to Circeto of the icy heights . . ." In a décor that is in itself enough to prohibit any simply libertine thoughts, I imagine this solemn and fugitive rendezvous. Above valleys that are deeper, blacker, more abrupt than the polar night, enormous mountain pinnacles packed together in the night, shoulder to shoulder under their cloak of forests—just as, in the "human pyramid" above the necks of young Atlases taut with effort, a gracious apparition, arms extended, seems to soar on the tip of a single foot— or even more like the celestial visitation of eternal snows in the light of day, their touch on each summit of glory in a Pentecostal light—the eye raised from under an impossible angle perceives in the midst of a nocturnal winter sky lighthouse beacons revolving amidst sarabands of snow, long, splendid vehicles slipping noiselessly along swept avenues where, sometimes, a glacier familiarly bares the incongruous whiteness of an enormous shoulder—and all full of sumptuous toys, calm children, thick furs, traveling at speed along the noble and interminable facades of *winter* palaces toward the nostalgic and mysterious Christmas of this capital of ice.

The delightful memory has stayed with me of that city where pink Bengal lights exploded among snow-covered hills, where at midnight gilded youth from the wealthy districts amused themselves by tossing into the precipices that surround this belvedere of ice flaming torches that shrank softly, regularly, in transparent blackness until, breath halted by a vague nausea, eyes were raised to the night pocked with cold stars and the planet was felt to pivot on that extreme point. In front of the casino steps two steep, majestic, immaculate avenues intersected a two-way bend; carriages with stalled engines hurtling like sleighs carried the last revelers home toward the pretty, vertical suburbs with the soft rhythm of aerolites, the electric lights, always so poor and shivery on the white streets, were enriched in my eyes with implications from beyond, with magnificent highlights in each fold of snow, more suspicious and, one might have thought, more laden with contraband corpses under that pestilential light than the plains of all the Russias.

But in the ice-cold air of four in the morning, the immense avenues empty under their flickering lights! A vague mist arose from the abysses and, complicit with the drowsiness of the extreme cold, merged the feeble lights of the valleys with the light of the stars. Leaning on a stone parapet, eyes on the cool and cloudy gulfs as moist in the mornings as a mouth, my reverie at last found a direction. On the vertiginous kilometers of these inordinate avenues, nothing could be heard save the murmur of arc lamps and the sharp cracking noise of the nearby glacier like an animal rattling its chain in the night. Sometimes, at the end of a prospect, a drunkard clambered over the ramp of a boulevard as though it were a gunwale.

Cities! Too loosely located!

And yet there's one real city that moves me to rapture; it's Saint-Nazaire that I want to talk about. On low ground, fronted by the sea, mined from behind by marshes, thrown on close-cropped grass that accentuates the vigorous ribs of the coasts of Brittany like the glossy hair of a beast, it's hardly more than a herd of white and gray houses awkwardly scattered like sheep on the moors, but more crowded at the center and as though huddled together in fear of the powerful battering of the sea winds. The approach to that town, which I've always imagined as being loosely tethered to the ground, ready to surrender to who knows what devious drifting movement, is really rather tragic. Thickets of giant cranes with horizontal arms rise like pinewoods above the muddy banks of this great gray northern river, in perpetual migration, calling on the whiteness of legendary swans like a redemption, becoming in a final melancholic avatar the mild and luminous river of Touraine.

Through the window of the railway carriage, one also dreams, caught in the lens of a periscope, of the landing site of Wells's giant tripods from Mars.

To it I owe the surprise, one fine summer day, of one of those poetic collusions, one of those *odd ideas* that sometimes arise in things, and suddenly banish the worst imaginings. Above the roofs of its low houses, the town, in I think profound mockery of its derisory terrestrial attachments, had, instead of the *nave* of its absent cathedral—thirty meters in height and more visible from ten leagues all round than the steeples of Chartres—hoisted the enormous hull of the liner "Normandy" between its blocks. A city, ocean-bound from everywhere, sailing like its sheet-metal cathedral, a city where, on the vague boulevard of mist that commands the open sea, between the fine geographies of a morning downpour on asphalt and soon dried, I've felt myself perfectly adrift like the mastless barge of the poet under his mild, adventurous sky.

But does it still exist, this Saint-Nazaire of which I dream in the depth of my room? It and so many others. Impossible cities like those built with opium, with smooth glacial facades, mute paving stones, pediments lost in the clouds, the cities of De Quincey and Baudelaire, dreamed Broadways with vertiginous granite trenches—De Chirico's hypnotic cities—built by Amphion's lyre, destroyed by the trumpets of Jericho—was it not inscribed for all time in the most touching of fables that your stones, hanging from the strings of the lyre, awaited only the most fragile of poetic inspirations in order to be set moving. It's to this myth, in which the inquisition of the most overwhelming constraints of heaviness is so lucidly made to depend on the purest breath of the spirit, that I would like to confide the secret hopes that I continue to nourish of not being the eternal prisoner of this squalid street of shops in which at the present moment for example I'm bound (!) to live.

Why shouldn't I cling to such thoughts in order to sometimes rouse myself to smile at their cities of stone and brick? They're free to think of *residing* there. After all, appearances are nothing to the devil, and, lame as he seemingly is, like justice, he'll never be finished with blowing up roofs.

VENICE

On that beach where the snow flew in concert with the light foliage of foam, in the five o'clock sunlight I rang at the gates of the Palazzo Martinengo. I was alone at the geometric center of this gigantic raised eyebrow of sand—a few minutes more and the dunes sounding the retreat would, with their blonde squadrons, shut me off from the passage to the waves. Like a Bastille Day celebration of flags and fireworks, the bell penetrated corridors sleepy as oil, bronze galleries with derisory pinchbeck armor, disturbing the treasure chest under a fold of shadow. At the rear, the pinewood was suddenly like the mineral illumination of spotlights during the orchestra's moonlight interlude in *Werther*. This, I told myself joyfully, was true solitude. Overhead, solemn as a stage flat, the shutter of a high window banged in the wind amidst a stampede of sand. The sea thundering from one end of the bay to the other abridged the conclusion of a dubious escapade. With my left hand I tried as delicately as possible to break the glass cover of one of those charming eighteenth-century caskets that sometimes mask the face of a fire alarm. When, in a concerted outburst, thirty bells bored like gimlets at the house's foundations, the spectacle that ensued can only be compared with a nocturnal panic on a transatlantic liner, an explosion of jazz drumming, a carnival of Last Judgment, and, with the majesty of a sounding line touching the bottom of the Philippines trench, the beard of the patriarch of the Adriatic descended toward me like the curtain of a window.

———————

The missed rendezvous of lovers in the hollow of a por-
phyry quarry—the Gehenna and the lunatic jig of ships
ablaze on a foggy night in the North Sea—the vast
bramble undergrowth and the high graveyard wreaths
of a bombed factory—can only give a faint idea of this
void flecked with burn marks, the downstream drift and
the devastation of wreckage like the swollen waters of
the Amazon in which my spirits haven't ceased to float
since the departure, amidst enigmatic monosyllables, of
her whom I was no longer able to name save with the
names of inaccessible glaciers, or certain splendid Mon-
golian rivers with singing reeds, with odorous white
tigers, with the tenderness of useless oases amidst the
burned gravel of the Steppes, those rivers that stream
so peacefully beside the song of a bird lost on top of a
reed, as though alighting there after the subsidence of
floods in a landscape swept clean of the last traces of
man; Nonni, Kerulen, Selenga. Nonni is the name I give
her in her gentle solicitude, her great vistas of tenderness
as though under convent veils, it's the pebbly softness

of her dry hands, her slight infant sweat, light as dew after the morning embrace, it's the little sister of nights innocent as lilies, the little girl of prudent games, of pillows white as a cool September morning—Kerulen is the red storms of her muscles stricken with fever, it's her mouth twisted by that devastating sculptural torsion of iron girders after a fire, the great green waves where her stormy legs float between the sea's cool muscles when I sink with her like a plank through translucent strata and this great noise of tolled bells that accompanies us on the deep seabed—Selenga is when her gown floats like a flight of sunlit seagulls in the midst of the empty morning streets, it's in the great fluttering sails, ocellated with her eyes like the trailing tail of a bird, those are her liquid eyes that swim about her like a dance of the stars—it's when she descends into my dreams down the calm chimneys of December, sits near my bed and takes my hand timidly between her small fingers for the difficult journey through the solemn landscapes of night, and, transparent to all the comets, her eyes open above mine till morning.

THE COLD WIND OF THE NIGHT

———————

In the evening I waited for her in the hunting lodge near the Morte River. The fir trees shook in the hazardous nighttime wind with the rustle of a shroud and the crackle of a conflagration. The black night was lined with ice, like white satin under an evening gown—curled hands ran in all directions on the snow outside. The walls were great dark curtains and, like lights glancing off frozen ponds, the mystical light of candles on the white sheets of the snowy steppes sprang up as far as the eye could see. I was the king of a people of blue forests, like an unmoving pilgrimage that lines up with its banners on the edge of a lake of ice. On the roof of the cave the cyclone of black thoughts shifted from time to time, as motionless as a fabric of watered silk. Leaning on the mantelpiece, wearing black tie and brandishing a revolver with a melodramatic gesture, for want of anything better to do I questioned the green and sleeping water of this ancient ice; a stronger gust occasionally misted it with a fine sweat like that of carafes, but I emerged once more, spectral and fixed, like a bridegroom on the photographic plate that surfaces from a swirl of green plants. Ah! The hollow hours of the night, like one who travels on the slight pneumatic bones of an express train—but suddenly there she was, sitting upright in her long white robes.

OPEN WATER

In that warm June afternoon, a cockcrow trails through empty streets where no one is to be found. Silence, deep as an abandoned hayloft, glutted with heat and dust. What indolence under the low vaults of the lime trees, on the doorknockers where a thousand bronze mouths are yawning! What a *distinguished* Sunday afternoon, evoking dreams of black gloves with lace cuffs on the arms of young girls, prudent parasols, inoffensive perfumes, arid steppes from five to seven! Only—like the dazzling swimmer who, swept along on the foam, suddenly casts a shadow of stupidity over the crowd planted on the beach—an alert little white cloud all at once covers the sleeping countryside with confusion and begets a dream of extravagance in a tree at the bottom of the avenue that has never yet taken flight.

GANG

Loaded right in the heart of this town, there has always been this district revolving like the barrel of a gun, intermittently shooting the torrent of its cars toward the suburban roads. It's from here that we went on our surprise journeys and the evenings bordered with eglantines, the fine mornings of trout fishing documentaries that stir whole fistfuls of gems in a salad bowl. Fingers grip the metal edging and the current of air carves an eagle's beak and the majesty of a figurehead under the helmet of white canvas. At the hem of white gowns on each boulevard black with oil, a forest that, like the Red Sea, opens in a gust of wind—in the enfilade of each sunlit puddle, the ingot of ice that cuts through the clumps of trees—at the tip of each branch, a flower that unfolds with a flapping of linen—at the end of each arm the burning rose of a revolver.

GRAND HOTEL

My people are a boisterous breed who more than any-
thing prefer the busy afternoons of a luxurious city
before an opera gala that solemnizes the day's longest
downward slope, the torrid afternoons when the sun
buzzes behind the thick forests of blinds unfurled on
the hotel's facade like a nautical fete, a white and proud
display of regatta bunting above the oily black asphalt
where the eaten-up reflection of puddles of leaves be-
comes flimsily unreal. I couldn't, without difficulty, spare
the luxury of any one of those details of bad taste that
mysteriously create its poetry; summer furs, melancholy
cascades of gratuities sounding along tombstone stairs,
smoking rooms with plumed voices stunned by Cordo-
van leather, nickel bars of sick-nurses from whence the
horizon flees toward the jetties—but, curled up in the
cushions at the bottom of a motor car in the heart of a
warm evening, luxury is, above all, a marvelously green
horizon dilated with nearby music, face upturned to a
sky as green as the meadows, the delicious wind of costly
speed spread evenly over the face, like the rediscovery of

fine simplicity, princely generosity, the ancient poverty of pure gold flowing between the fingers.

———

God, how tedious, being condemned to this curse of thickness. This body like a livid goatskin bag, decaying like everything possessing a stomach, and all human servitude in that word, a word that decapitates the stars, the most derisory, the most buffoonish word in the language, *gravitate*. Nothing has ever upset me so much as the smiling avatar of promise at the foot of my bed, a person become a mirror in his plush frame—and, no doubt at the heavy finish of a secret of divine sloth, dissolved in the plane surface and entrusted to the most consoling of mediators which for me is the infinite. Can one ever live in any other way than *thin-skinned*, get caught in traps other than those of mirrors and—spread out like those fine ox-hides that imbibe the sun through all their length—smooth, unwrinkled, like virgin wax on the threshold of great nocturnal signs—a dried bouquet releasing its memories in the dark—in front of that yellowing photograph in its plush frame, have I ever been able to slip between the pages of my bed, tarot card shuffled in the game of dream, without musing on the day when—ageless as a playing card king—as familiar as the graceful double of Egyptian bas-reliefs—as flat as the ancestor at the bottom of the lead mine, the guillotined man's beautiful shirt, family albums—bereft of bones like those handsome racing car fatalities heartbroken from having awoken too soon in the hollow of a splendid dream of levitation—I'll return to haunt my perfect image.

THE SLEEPY GARDEN

———

What tranquility now that the noonday chimes make the day slide insensibly down its most tragic slope. The complicated pear trees, as hard and branching as corals, the asters, the mille-feuilles, the St. John's wort grow through seedbeds of oyster shells, and the pretty pebbles form pathways of pleasure, gentle routes between lawns like the contour of a breast. Behind the mossy wall the sea, like a tumbled automobile, stands at a forty-five-degree angle, gray as the beautiful tonality of the planet seen from Sirius, truly restful—the fundamental sea, both judge and jury.

ISABELLE ELIZABETH

The singularity of *Isabelle's* face was made from the various whitenesses of linen, those dazzling stretches of calm sea between two tidal currents, those beaches friendly to the sleek light of a July afternoon on a slate roof. A choice neck made for the noble harnesses of a war horse, her breasts fixed like pegs for climbing a beautiful tree, the hold they invited with two open and welcoming hands, eyes complicated and prehensile like the tendril of a sweet pea, desires as brutal and wanton as a wave battering a jetty on a day of the most glorious weather, I remember all that like it was yesterday. Above all else, I admired her flair for ambiguity—her hands change like the wind, the world places her smooth feet on I don't know what resounding hurricane of tiles, and, singular as those transmutations encouraged by a Prince Charming's lifted eyebrow on seeing the embraces of Beauty and the Beast, it's suddenly from a *lost profile* of that strange figure against a background of forests and changing leaves—mad and always attentive to I don't know what lost memory—that the beauty of *Elizabeth's* face is made.

THE ROSS BARRIER

———

You have to get up early in the morning to see the day dawning on the horizon of the ice floe, at that hour when the sun of the southern latitudes stretches up from the sea roads. Miss Jane carried her umbrella, and I an elegant double-barreled shotgun. We kissed each other in mint crevasses at the defile of each glacier and happily prolonged the moment to see the sun's red cannonballs open a path through a Chantilly cream of sparkling ice. We preferred to go by way of the seashore where the soft elephantine roll of the cliff, breathing regularly with the tide, inclined us to lovemaking. The waves beat against the glacier's walls of blue and green snow and scattered giant crystal flowers at our feet in the cove, but above all, the approaching day was responsive to that slight phosphorescent rim traced on their scalloped edge, as when nocturnal capitals take to sailing on the slack water of their high seas. Edelweiss the color of midnight blue grew in the fissures of the ice at Cape Disappointment, and we were always sure of seeing a fresh supply of seabird eggs, daily replenished, and which, so Jane believed, had the virtue of lightening the complexion. Plucking that childish adage from Jane's mouth with my lips was for me a daily repeated ritual. Sometimes the clouds, concealing the floor of the cliff, foretold an overcast sky in the afternoon and Jane inquired mildly if I'd carefully wrapped the Cheshire cheese sandwiches. At last the cliff reached higher, all chalky with sun; it was Point Desolation and, on a sign from Jane, I spread the blanket on the cool snow. We lay there for a long time, listening to the beating breasts of the sea's wild horses in the ice caverns. The horizon of the open sea was a semi-circle of diamond blue under which lay the wall of ice where sometimes a cloud of steam formed, floating up from the sea like a white veil—and Jane recited Lermontov's stanzas for me. I would have spent entire afternoons there, my hand in hers, following the cawing of seabirds and throwing bits of ice that we listened to as they fell into the abyss while Jane counted the seconds, poking out the tip her tongue in concentration, like a schoolgirl. Then our embrace was so long and close that a single trough was hollowed out in the melted snow, narrower than a child's cradle, and when we got up, the blanket between the white mounds brought to mind those Asian mules coming down from the mountains saddled with snow.

The sea then turned a deeper blue and the cliff became violet; it was that time of day when those crystal burgs that crumble into a dust of ice are broken off from the ice floe by the brusque cold of the evening with the

JULIEN GRACQ

sound of a world exploding, and, under the cyclopean spiral of a blue wave, upend the belly of a passenger ship rough with dark seaweed, or the heavy snorting of a bath of plesiosaurs. For us alone that end-of-the-world cannonade gradually lit up the horizon to its far edge, like a Waterloo of the spaces of solitude—and for a long time yet the great silence of the frozen nightfall was pierced by the ghosts of high, white-plumed geysers spurting in the distance—but I'd already gripped Jane's ice-cold hand in mine, and we returned by the light of the pure Antarctic stars.

THE DOWNPOUR

Here's the world brooding under the rain, the muggy heat, the roof of twigs and droplets, and the soft blankets of air with a thousand tingling splashes. Here's the beautiful woman on her bed of water, entirely awoken by the sudden cool transparence, entirely at one with a pure idea of herself, entirely defined as water is by glass. In the air where stuttering stars of water are swimming, a hand of air emerges from the alcove green with herbal perfumes to hang, tied back with lianas, the beaded curtains and the crackling arithmetic of the crystal abacus.

JULIEN GRACQ

VERGISS MEIN NICHT

What are you doing at this late time of night? Perhaps sitting sewing by the happy light of diligent evenings, of careful hands, of the mushrooming desire for good work that loosens tongues for benevolent chatter under the lamp, and the warm, happy thoughts that are dispensed all round to the friendly absent one—perhaps, at the window in front of a wood of fir trees under the brilliant moon, the moist fingers of your hand touch the great mineral cold that prowls between the planets, and you think that I'm far away, behind that horizon where a train disappears, feathered with its soft lights, drunk on its metallic clangor in the calm night—perhaps a book betrays me through the beating fan of those pages turned in the fever of a gentle breeze of hair, and misfortunes overwhelm you when suddenly nothing would seem to you unhealthier than me with no part to play—or else in the room where you fall sleep, where suddenly everything abandons me and you flow amidst your dreams in the exhilaration of being so alone, and, steered by the mysterious clues of the following morning, delightedly contrive a whole hive of bad bees for the nocturnal thieves.

UNAPPROACHABLE

It's a young woman from under whose feet images arise in profusion. On an April path she sometimes raises a hand as soft and gentle as a quill pen and, as though reluctantly, soothes the landscape's anxieties—or else the mysterious calligraphy of her walk between the asphalt margins competes with it for the littérateur's most exquisite instrument. In the meanderings of a colorful street, I love to follow the thread of that melody of sudden death sent echoing from end to end of the horizon of facades by her arrival. What street sound—from a devastated theater, smashed shop windows, newspaper vendors shouting the supreme murder of the century, what blood-red trinkets, what beautiful blood foaming and warbling like arpeggios, like trills, what soft saxophone inflection would ever equal for me the look that she pours from the corner of her precise and calm eye, the magnetic stream of her gaze that flows in full spate between the houses like the acid saliva of a glacier?

HANSEATIC CITIES

Awakening of a young beauty lying on the grass near a city, in front of the glittering of water and the laziness of ten o'clock, under the blue-tinted light. The belfries and turrets of that time-worn city, its streets high and narrow for the riots of the roaring crowd starved by sieges, the mall's sumptuous trees overshadowing the ostentatious jewels, smothering the proud velvet and closing a snood of sun on young women's hair on days of triumph and parades, and the triangular plazas with their potent stink of filth under the cruel sun. Like a blue river, the air flows and washes the bridges in musical spirals. The noble little city indents a steep slope of dream on the horizon, beyond a field of festivities divided by a stream, but all the warm light serves to deepen the aroma of a stifling head of hair on mown hay, and to hemstitch a naked foot and hand whose fingers play the complicated strings of the air.

FURNISHED SALON

In the very dark day—with the specially sinister tonality that filters through the closed blinds of a mortuary chamber on a scorching August afternoon—down walls painted with that translucent glaze that coats stalactite caves, viscous to the eye but hard as glass to the touch, a slight, noiseless ribbon of water, rippling as over the slates of a urinal, shimmers, soft as silk. The rivulets, merging in a half-light at the left angle of the room, nourish a little bed of watercress before making their escape. Over on the right, in a big lightning-proof Faraday cage, flung negligently over the arm of a curule seat as though after a morning stroll, Caesar's bloody toga recognizable by its museum label and the *sui generis* aspect of particularly authentic slashes in the material. A rustic Swiss clock with two tones, cuckoo and quail, sounds the quarter and half hours for the aquarium silence. On the mantelpiece, amidst a profusion of *much* more sumptuous bibelots, victims of I don't know what specially prearranged display, an open packet of Scaferlati tobacco and a photograph of President Sadi-Carnot at his first communion (stiff cardboard, dog-eared, thick and gilt-edged, serious effort for Catholic families, signed by the photographer). In the shadowy rear of the salon, a turreted goods wagon on its siding, lightly sprinkled with daisies and umbellifers, lets the gleam of a Sevres China service and a fine array of little liqueur glasses filter through its open door.

A HIBERNATING MAN

On awakening in the morning, the double windows imprisoned him in the virgin forest of their delicate fronds of ice. An overnight film of moisture was all it needed to burgeon. However, walking upside down was hardly cause for surprise; the sky was no more than dirty gray mold while the Milky Way of the snow lit up the world from below. All the faces were beautiful, rejuvenated—the snow gave birth to glorious bodies. At noon, standing on one foot and holding his breath, he fine-tuned the silence in the garden of cotton wool and snow. In the evening the fluffy labyrinth of the fog locked and chained the house—doors still swung on their hinges. Then the rays of the moon prowled around the room until the window placed a big black cross on the bed. These delicate, luminous frauds weren't always free from danger, though.

Like the figurehead of a three-deck ship gone astray in this port of galleys above the flat Mediterranean the white of whose waves always seem exhausted by an excess of salt, the face of that violent woman surged up for me from behind an impeccably correct row of tumblers of alcohol. At the rear were the great melancholy pines, the direction of whose branches filter out almost everything except the sun's horizontal rays at that sunset hour when the roads are pure, beautiful, surrendered to the song of fountains. The sound of hammers on hulls came audibly from the depth of the port, infinite, tireless, like a *chanson de toile* above an artless tapestry frame swept by two blonde tresses, surrounded by an endless web of domestic cares, with at its center those two gentle eyes, tired under the curls, the sister, no less, of inexhaustible fountains. One never tires of drinking, a liquid clear as glass, a singing morning alcohol. But in the end it was a good and proper bout of lassitude, and suddenly, as though the *permitted* hour had been exceeded—the port taken by surprise under that forbidden light when, thanks to a curtain of mist, the handsome pirates of the northern night, the Breton washerwomen, unexpectedly swoop down in a hit-and-run raid—suddenly it was the murmur of the poplar trees and the bite of moist cold—then the banging of a door and it was the exit from theaters in the white nights of St Petersburg, it was an array of unimaginable furs, the hard and milky opacity of the Baltic—in a dawn soiled with coarse spittle, prolonged by unreal chandeliers, the street that pours a troika out on the sea-facing cliffs, a mournful infinity of gray swells like a doomsday—it was already time to go to the Islands.

ROBESPIERRE

The angelic beauty that in spite of ourselves we attribute—beyond the dusty pages of a book never browsed through save in fever—to some of the lesser terrorists; Saint-Just, Jacques Roux, Robespierre the Younger—the beauty that preserves them for us through the centuries, the nickname of the Incorruptible swimming around a garland of graceful decapitated heads like an Egyptian balm—the whiteness of those necks of Jean-Baptiste sharpened by the guillotine, the ebullitions of lace, the white gloves and yellow breeches, the bouquets of ears of corn, the hymns, the breakfast in the sun before the Revolutionary ceremonies, the blondness of ripening wheat, the flexible curve of mouths sticky with a dream of death, the cooing of Jean-Jacques under the somber verdure of the first chestnut boughs of May, green as never before with the beautiful red blood of the guillotine blades, the funereal madrigals of sleepwalking Brummells, a bunch of periwinkles held in the hand, this collapse of flowers, of virginal aristocrats into the basket of bran—as though, in the knowledge of being one day carried alone on the end of a pike, all of the fascinating beauty of the night of man must have flooded the magnetic features of those medusa heads—that superhuman chastity, that ascesis, that wild beauty of the cut flower that makes every woman pale in the face—it's the tongue of fire that, for me, descends mysteriously here and there amidst silhouettes as rapid as the lights of great streets moving as though on the screen of an alley of trees ablaze in the countryside on a June night, and with a certain panicked ecstasy points out to me the unforgettable face of a certain few guillotined from birth.

———————

A big palace with clouded corridors—perspectives of sun and mist at the front, the morning plainsong of sun on the fog banks ripped by the tops of lighthouses, an everlasting November of dulcet showers of rain, of stray birds that clear the seas with a single cry—at the back, a residential lawn with an aviary and a view of the gasometer—I retired there for weeks on end, for holiday leisure, picnics, one only multiplied as by a play of mirrors, as by trompe l'oeil perspectives. The twists and turns of the coastal roads accommodated this special *day* of monuments pummeled by the tides. By way of furniture, nothing but sextants, celestial spheres, buckled astrolabes, and in general everything that might disturb a brain dwelling on the oppressive forecast of a succession of days all too closely aligned with the calendar's index. On days of blinding sunlight a tapestry of mist was spread out over the spars, the fine laundry of long-haul three-masters hung out to dry from the architectural upright of ornamental moldings, a wealth of batiste as heavy as brocade, phantom awnings and, as enormous as the hull's varnished cupboard, wellspring of the giant shrouds of good weather, the swollen, pot-bellied palace navigated the space between the planets, an ether fertilized by broad white breasts, by cloth cumuli, by a flapping maelstrom of whiteness, the gigantically indecent loosening of bridal veils.

THE TRUMPETS OF AIDA

Great secret landscapes as intimate as dream, ceaselessly wheeled round and evaporated on her like the light incense of clouds on the incandescent tip of a mountain peak. Her coming was like the luminous face of a forest contemplated from a tower, like the sun dissipating the mists of a rainy coast, like the uplifting song of the trumpet on the enlarged courtyards of the morning. Near her I sometimes dreamed of a barbarian horseman with a conical cap straddling his dwarf horse like a rigid church bench, all alone and with the tiny trot of a mechanical toy crossing the Mongolian steppes—and at other times it was some old emperor called Bulgaroktonos, like a parchment reliquary borne into Saint Sophia for Thanksgiving while the bone-colored stones of Byzantium sink under the centuries-old grass and the superhuman orgasm of the trumpets paralyze the setting sun.

No, that's not what I came for, if it's what bothering you. Forget it. What's the use!—don't make a scene—we understand each other better than you think. That idea came to me while you were sleeping *the sleep of the just*. It's an odd expression—let's admit it—but I took as needed from somewhere other than the failings of language, and such peculiar nighttime outpourings aren't an open book for me to read. There's nothing there that can hurt you.

I found then lost myself again in the corridors of this theater, like a needle in a haystack.

I dreamed I'd met a strikingly beautiful woman. You're laughing already, you don't think you can stomach such a farcical allegory. But I'm older than you think.

You thought you were on your own in going to such culpable extremes, but a figure of speech kept you company.

I have this power. But in another minute, it'll be too late. The chance of a light behind an open door that slams shut the moment of passing it by, very late, in these hotel corridors in an unknown city where everything bewilders. Of course, one never goes inside.

This morning I had the pleasure of saying hello to the poet Francis Jammes at the steering wheel of his steam cylinder.

You have no secrets for me. The locks you fasten here and there on the dubious doors through which you make your escape? I've *also* recovered from rash acts and doors that slam shut on a monotonous circuit, like the museum rooms where everything comes back to the upshot of the wearisome carnival merry-go-round. No, I only wanted to talk about that odd voice, *a little* too shrill—tense if you prefer—that you adopted that weekend last June to tell me about your trip in an overcrowded compartment. For a long time that rather piping tone of voice lessened the intensity of the day by a degree for me, even if I sometimes came across it again in the twists and turns of an aimless conversation for which, I must admit, you have a distinct talent. What nonsense.

I knew a house where *petits fours* were served in rose leaves—but all the same, it's too much, much too much.

These are such big words. But on leaving Lucien at the theater door, I thought that your behavior was odd. It's true that the conversation got off to a bad start. Lucien is delightful. In every way. But you're flustered.

I've got two big oxen in my stable. That might be surprising—but after all it only has value as a *simple observation*.

Reading Mauriac's latest novel brought Hélène to mind. Don't you think so? All those upsets considerably shortened the life of her mother.

We have a little chat in the corridors of the metro, when I go down to empty my toilet bucket.

No, nothing. It was an idea. You'll laugh. But, just like adolescents visiting well-kept museums to dream preferably about the solution to a humble technical problem—I've often found myself contemplating a statue of Joan of Arc, or the photograph of a shrimper girl—always captivated beyond measure by the absorbing image of a woman made taller by the standard she bears.

The day breaks in a rain of sheet lightning, greeted by maternal snowfall. The assembly line worker, skilled at reckoning the soft flow of the minutes with his index finger, suddenly imagines a particular remission of his dream and falls asleep. The connecting rods and drive belts are suddenly sprinkled with primroses. The world dozes, scarcely time enough to sneeze an *Ave Maria*.

This canal under the dazzling February light. Small waves at the foot of the clifftop avenue make the blue of the water unbearable, like the rough impasto of a painting. Those beautiful Renaissance windows in front of the Yacht Club's noble pavilion, the long quay, the tossing of the skiffs, and, at the rear, the vague nothingness of suburban meadows between the railway embankments, like green jaws open in a vast yawn— with those beautiful electricity pylons between which the angels walk the tightrope every time the starting gun turns the heads of the spectators. Very nice.

In the salons of Calm Beach Residence, on the evening of the Fleurie Redoute, the stately scandal of that bridge party where, backed into a corner by an exorbitant bid, an individual in an evening suit and wearing a black mask, leaning over on my left, casually slipped this *nine of asparagus* into my sleeve at the last moment, securing me a grand slam.

My most delicate memories? Those solitary evenings in the rendezvous of the Black Forest hunt. A great fire of top hats lit up my nights; "So, another moonlit night," I sometimes mused, leaning on a bit of candelabrum—"there'll be a mass embarkation from the Drum-Major's dock."

In the clear polar nights, I've sometimes hunted, if only to feel their avian triggers under my fingers, those frozen and burning shrimps that ascend from dark caves and congregate in clusters at the edge of crevasses to see the sparkling of the Southern Cross.

THE SUSQUEHANNA RIVER

———————

Goods trains roll all along the Susquehanna River in winter, and the engine drivers with their pretty madapolam caps patronize a row of little cottages on the Dutch riverbanks. Silent ballets are sometimes completed by skaters in front of the pearly breathed air vent of a railway wagon numb with snow on its siding—but from dawn to dusk the overriding impression is of a carillon of big wooden bells. The noonday light in the blizzard and its soot-sprinkled cotton is an indifferent Siberian dawn, with the crash of sawn logs and the humming noise of canvas lift shafts—uncertain distances reveal, at ten meters, a whistling crewman, hands in pockets, crossing a siding. Sleepwalkers smelling of wet dog are grouped out of the way in a waiting room blinded by a stove. Each seems to ignore his neighbor, and the sleepy comings and goings espouse nothing more than a purely formal propriety in awaiting, as in the theater, the six o'clock bell, with the fine-looking black groups who drift away in the snow. There are also the abandoned sheds where steaming grogs are downed in an odor of tar and

Christmas trees like a mouthful of fresh sawdust, and the little bars in the wilderness of rail tracks, with removable panels around a color lithograph of Trotsky receiving the German parliamentarians in front of the Brest-Litovsk railway station.

FINE MORNING STROLL

My morning stroll scarcely under way, I was sometimes caught off guard barely a few cables' length from my room by a dissonant crashing of copper proceeding from the demolition of a graceful little brick house. On the selected themes of that mysterious fanfare of the ruins I imagined, behind the sad facade of plaster rubble, an entire theory of artless morning bowers in which electricians in red overalls, blondes walking the dawn pavements, serious professional processions *en travesti* facing the sunrise dispelled their nocturnal fog within themselves, in some of those fancy pewter mugs that figure to such effect in the foreground of an opera buffa bacchanal. Can you imagine anything more charming, before the hasty departure for work, under the braid trim and the pleasant constellations of boiler suits, than the fresh chorus of the dewdrops, fanned by expired candelabra, lifted up to the sun by those ingenuous stagehands condemned to simulate ruffians for the entire day in the dustiest wings of a modern city? A minute-ball, the flight of a lace petticoat in the dog and wolf of dawn was the limit of such scandals as I was able to imagine in that tiny enclosure concealed from sidewalk surveyors by the conventional collapse of a plaster curtain wall under a demolition worker's three hammer blows. But already a pretty tavern of badly carpentered beams allowed its shutters to sing in the dawn sunlight, like joyful garden insects opening their morning wings. Already the welcoming street was calling me; in a great array the paving stones were repositioned in their honeycomb patterns—after all, nothing had happened—and, like a black velvet mask on a wantonly debauched woman's most disturbing face, the streetlights and the wobbling rubbish bins, after their balletic morning leap, resumed their shared guard duty under the military eye of the municipal street sweepers.

THE GREAT GAME

That *je ne sais quoi* of insubstantiality that hovers over districts near railway stations—the fertility of the great white clouds of June over green meadows, their edges consumed by azure like the blue veins that become milk in a breast—that tender dewy glaze in the eyes and on the lips, that navel of Venus Anadyomene in whose mother-waters the most moving of women for me will always bathe—water and leaves suddenly bristling in the powdery light of a misty summer morning along the recumbent meadows and the willows of great rivers—the heart's sudden pang before the solemn landscape of clearings, more poignant between the margins of assembled forests than the still virgin field of battle, the prodigious concert of silence that separates two armies before the trumpet sings—that tender flowering rose, that effusion of petals which, in the heart of metal red hot for me alone, awakens the great sheet-metal flags, the immaculate metal stamp of arums and lilies—the sudden twilight, the melancholy *petite mort* of bells in the afternoons stunned by Sunday suns—the great sphinxes

that, at twilight, stretch out over the misty ponds of sta-
diums—the brow as far as the eye can see over the plains
of a legendary woodland like the wall of a cataract of si-
lence—at the twelfth stroke of midnight the forbidden
phantom of a gold and purple theater, glazed, nacreous,
partitioned, laminated like a shellfish, deserted as a ter-
mite mound after the ritual slaughter of the royal cou-
ple in a maelstrom of claws and pincers—the delirious
Euclidean geometries of marshaling yards—the majestic
processions of furniture of a former era, the big trans-
ports of goods train box-beds—the middle-distance run-
ner, his sovereign face, closed and sealed like a piece of
marble, suspended above a bend in the road like a man
who plunges into the sea on horseback—the abundant
manchineel trees of Venetian chandeliers—the charm
of the redundant forests in the vicinity of Paris, where
sometimes a single *water tower* watches over immense
solitudes—I've sometimes dreamed of *turning over* these
obsessional images, these tarots of a crooked card game—
to seek for whom these figures, for me always singular,
could only be the same on both sides.

THE BASILICA OF PYTHAGORAS

That lively city that as yet I've no wish to enjoy is there in a corner of my memory. The boulevards turn with the sun's rays and the shadows are forever restricted to the side streets and the run-down neighborhood of the conspirators. It's there, after midday, that I make my way through lanes where the grass bends under the constant wind. Here and there antiquated hotels with stone baldachinos are jumbled together with some of those charming disused rural railway stations that have been swallowed up by the city in passing—no less well preserved, indeed, than Jonah in his whale. At the corner of the street the tarnished first-class waiting room sign sways in the breeze. Here, a hospitable house hosts its sportive games—and why not? I've sometimes come across by no means deplorable goings-on in the hollow of a bundle of cotton beside the ticket booth. In an apotheosis of colored madras cloth and that shadow—that cool shadow!—you suddenly think yourself in the heart of South Carolina! And the dust!—that fine coal dust of weathered railway stations that smell so intoxicatingly.

All around, a welcoming garden, autumn crocuses, bougainvillea. A prolonged stay is prohibited. The shadow of an all-white skyscraper smothers the little station, suddenly putting one in mind of Sicily, of the cliff-like streets of I don't know which concrete Salerno where, in a storm of flies, the shadows from the loggias of the town hall perched on high crush the port dwellings and their beautiful multicolored lingerie, their big heraldic shields on feast days, which are every day. There's also an orgy of iron clocks like big spiders. So tranquil, so debonair. The immense rattling of a streetcar penetrates the heart of all that like an earthquake, an explosion of crockery, or the cheerful din of tuned metal tubes set jingling by the doors of shops full of shadows where you haggle over wickerwork trinkets, chinaware, latticed phials of exotic perfumes. To return to the little station, a cedar tree has taken refuge in its garden. Between the vertical walls that it touches, and whose smooth poise makes the heart jump with joy, it spreads its branches like those stagnant water levels in very deep pits in years of drought. It had to be lowered down there at the end of a rope, and it's in that borehole, under that bed of verdure, under those valves of verdure dominated by one hundred and thirty-five floors and the new brightness of all the stars in broad daylight, it's there that I arrange my assignations, and my greedy kisses, my first kisses.

THE HANGING GARDENS

I entered the cool night of the chestnut trees. It's always near the outskirts of provincial towns, at the sudden insertion of derelict industrial zones where bundles of yarn, discarded underwear like *parietaria judaica* along leprous window gratings, shiver in the wind in a silence more chilling than that of a riot before the first shot rings out, that I like to follow through low black arches those trails that long remain moist on asphalt where pink and white petals cling tepidly to the ground, and those masses of damp air under the most impenetrable tunnel of branches that I've ever seen. Over on the right, the emptiness of pavements intercepted by falling trees is as surprising as a stretch of seawater and, depending on the slope, you can walk alone toward the sad rivers, the graveyard all through winter of pleasure crafts, of piazzas silently invaded by turf and the soundless games of the children of the poor, and sometimes a sluggish goods wagon or the derisory vocalise of a kite. In the outlying boulevards nothing moves me more than the terrace of a drowsy café smothered in black foliage. The solitude is that of the populated peripheries where you turn your shoulder to the windows—just like the gaze nearly sick with vertigo that, from the cliff-top of an overcrowded velodrome, floats over the no-man's land where drying linen hangs from the nomads' jalopies, or suburban marshaling yards incomprehensibly surrendered to lethargy. The hours slipping by effortlessly on the feathery dial of an oceanic sky between the leaves and leaving no trace, the colorless driving rain from which nothing is protected, the empty room, the domestic yawn that effortlessly submerges the bar—what a stopping point!—and to go nowhere, vertiginously, along those singular ring roads, disorientedly harassed as though by the trade wind of those great atolls of foliage, feeling, unmoving, this network of sudden death moving round the flank of the city, and those intimate troughs of wind, great spear thrusts of the desert reaching the threatened heart of the cities.

THE AMBIGUOUS EMBARKATION

At midnight, under moonlight sharp as a razor, I un-moored the funeral barge—and set sail. Long stretches of flat land, flights of ghostly wood pigeons white against the banks, it was the first awakening of the en-chanted waterway that I improvised in the hollow of the nocturnal landscape. On the banks, solemn and funereal knights with sable heraldic bearings greeted me with the blazing fleur-de-lis of their banners—an oriflamme hedge on water blue as petrol outlined the career open to the victor. Waves on the horizon lost themselves in big peaks—sometimes a fervent waterspout, a crystal gaunt-let, a pointed finger like the gnomon of a sundial, rep-resented the familiar zodiac of these ill-defined journeys. With suddenly brightened lanterns, the watery pan-demonium of a nocturnal embarkation, a thousand St. Elmo fires glowing on the rigging, I could detect breezes like the breath of a damp cellar approaching from the open sea, then it was a friendly nudge from the oil tank-ers, immense booms of mist, the giant handrails where the majestic bit players leaned for the send-off, with their snow-white beards, their tail coats and theatrical fans, the black and salty splashes of soot where marble shoulders shivered and, already carried on the collar of the first swell and suddenly on a firm footing, the relief bugle call saluted the overflow on the jetty.

LANDSCAPE

Prey to the singular feeling of indolence that coincides with eating solitary meals at dusk, I'd arrived that evening at the big display board of the Western Cemetery. Only the clear furrows of fields of cereal crops, the disparate avenues hollowed out by the transient emotions of the Mediterranean, are able to rival those solemn alignments of tombs that span the rolling hills, and which, in industrial zones, are sometimes allowed to stultify a corner of the landscape under their crusts of stone like a Baltic Sea under pack ice. It was as though a gorgon of the fields had cast a spell on the beautiful shivering hair of the planet, the unmoving stone thistles, the granite stumps, the stubs of sawn tree trunks, the field of felled trees by the funeral chapels, their demented bric-a-brac furnishing a Canadian clearing deserted by the field-clearers at that time of day when the good evening soup is steaming in the pot. The illusion was only heightened here and there by a forgotten ax, a great array of spades near a freshly dug ditch. Briar patches entangled with treacherous strands of wire, suddenly it was also all the music of bombings, when the airy landscape, eased by a playful breath, allows a momentary relaxation of the laws of gravity—anyway, a rummage in the unpredictability of those odd trash cans was no doubt permitted, one was even astonished by the absence of the early morning poodle wagging its tail around the dustbin. From somewhere behind a hill a bugler sounded a disillusioned stink of the barrack-room, one of those solemn brass diminuendos that rhyme so well with the carefree growth of grass between paving stones, of daisies between tombstones, and, in the corner where the stelae are found, a little suburban salesgirl hunted for the first violets.

JUSTICE

An occasional nervous tic in my left shoulder, I listened unflaggingly to the pleas. A spider in the middle of the tribunal bobbed up and down on the end of its thread, like a complicated theater chandelier. Let me tell you, there wasn't anyone who didn't get the allusion; you could have heard a fly buzz. The flapping sleeves of the professionals spread a perfume of bitter almonds. Finally I found something odd about that, I wouldn't go as far as to say *sui generis*. One of them was condemned to death, three to life imprisonment, the others slipped out on tiptoe, with big theatrical gestures behind an elegant trompe-l'oeil of lace ruffles. When the curtain was raised for the third time, I was the only one in the room to thank the presiding judge, who spat cherry pips into his cap. Believe me, it was confusing.

JULIEN GRACQ

THE TRAVELING LIFE

―――――――

We left the town near three in the morning, when night owls are launched once more from the avenue's murky houses, facade after facade, like a silk cushion pigeon shoot. The day dawned in a ribbon of blue light on the rails of a suburban tramway—but well before the promised land the sky changes! It's rain on the windows of a derelict beachfront hotel, a breakfast of brown bread over which the sea makes a sound of weeping. Who to blame? We paced up and down the pier, utterly disoriented, perplexed, throwing our pieces of bread into the sea. So: I've now thrown the pauper's cape over my shoulders, retied my shoelaces at the bitter corner of a boundary, and all alone now under the gutter's gullet, I'm waiting for the grocery shops to open.

TRURO

The spires of Truro Cathedral are now two compact stonework cones, and while the look of the facades might be unchanged, the space is strangely measured by rooms prey to an abnormal thickening of the walls; as for the populace—the twisted and mean smile of someone whose foot has been trodden on—it's like a hermit crab driven from its shell by an internal tumor. Truro continues to suffer uncomplainingly. Year after year, the growth of mineral sap shrinks the available space toward the middle of the rooms; simultaneously, the sly war waged by vegetal genius against sharply defined angles is plain to see; already a quantity of dining rooms have become rounded and when invited by the town's polite society I've often had the anachronistic impression of taking tea in a dungeon. Any furnishings one hasn't taken the precaution of shifting are stuck fast to the walls by the progress of the vitreous coating which, due to its ganglionic appearance, isn't unlike those mucilaginous layers that, in cold winters, burgeon on the slate surface of urinals. Hangings in particular are rapidly affected by mineralization; they still look flexible, but a touch of the hand crumbles the fringes of the curtains into a friable chalk dust. Well might you shift your bed away from the walls and conceal your fears by pretending to the old-fashioned style of *centrally placed beds*, it nevertheless sometimes happens that, in the early morning, the visitor touches a bedsheet that's already rigid, or shatters an insidious marble film with an impatient toe, the way the flick of a fish's tail punctures the thin ice of southern seas. The phenomenon of stalactites is rarely seen save in rainy seasons in the vicinity of the Maritime District. It's not that there's any threat of danger, properly speaking, although subacute phenomena have already been observed, and instances of the accelerated blocking of emergency exits, and yet—while, I admit, without possessing *really* authoritative reasons—I now take the liberty of advising against a stay in Truro, for, as the poet remarks, such rooms are the dwelling place not only of the body, but also the imagination.

THE CONVENT OF THE PANTOCRATOR

Under the beautiful leaves of its palm trees the convent of the Pantocrator glistens like a woman centering herself before orgasm. Attempting the climb is difficult, and yet those serpentine rooms like meandering paths, those roofs streaked by the sun's oil, those varnished roofs, those butter roofs, that labyrinth of fig trees, of luminous splashes at the tip of a vertical precipice, that and that alone is what draws me, and toward which that tartan sets its sails on a sea as flat as a sound of surf. Hear the wind's felucca on the ridge pieces, the wind as slow as the waves—then it's the soft rain on the lead-latticed tiles, the silvery rain, the domestic rain between bright shelves of crockery and the family dog kennel, it's the convent on which the hours turn, the grisaille of hours, the clock of pastimes on which suns turn and on which the sea festoons its waves, the tongue protruding with the diligence of an embroiderer, of a seated and tranquil Penelope, of a village poisoner between her welcoming vials and the household bread she slices—the bread that supports and relaxes—the bread that nourishes.

ON THE BANK OF THE BEAU BENDÈME

Many a time I'd wandered in the waning hours of the afternoon through the cool lanes of the neighborhood of graveyards and riots bordering the mixed cathedral. At each of the buildings' blind spirals an emphatic nonchalance burdened my walk, like ringed fingers discreetly tapping a jewel box in the twilight of the beautiful Merovingian salons of antique dealers. The transparent prison of air retailed the sonority of gongs. Only here and there was I allowed some respite by worm-eaten benches that underlined the funereal stations of a *via crucis* emblazoned with Roman signs and phalerae, as complicated as the map of the subway. For what half-blind Calvary was this labyrinth the pedestal, for what suburban Babel? Doors sometimes slammed mysteriously, but it was always beyond a bend in the road, and in this foul sesame of the suburbs I almost itched with excitement at the deceptive pursuit. Those cries as grave as horns, this anxious pursuit through rubble clearings, those scaffoldings of ladders, an entire Hoggar calcined with blind shops that suddenly brought me, behind the sieves of a fine rain, into the presence of the *apse* of the most ambiguous building that I've ever been given to see—slipped me the password that placated the sentry at his post, and under the great smooth and sea-green lanterns of the windows, with tears in my eyes, I felt myself melting from the waist down in the muscular and shaggy grass of an oceanic meadow.

THE CLANDESTINE PASSENGER

Sometimes I was conveyed on the exorbitant shore of a glorious city, its sails bent to the air of its thousand masts, crying in the air its congealed stone cries like an exhausted geyser, a high pyramid of silkily glazed walls where in the evening streets the noble crystal of sonorous air found itself like a mirror above the sea ice, and, far beyond the high walls, calm trumpets incessantly safeguarded a mysterious solemnity—a seaport washed by winds and laid waste by a sea into which the rapid reddening suns plunged, and there, lying at the end of a mole, level with the waves all aslant and running furled together by a single gust of wind carrying off—on my shoulders, the towers and gilded domes smoldering with dust from the sun in the worn-out azure under the yoke of the warm day—fascinated by a dream salted with solar spindrift, and on my back the enormous swollen bubbles of those secular shells, the corridors of crime of those millions of alveolae, the deserted squares around the statues of glory and the ghosts of broad daylight, the doorways of blind palaces black-plumed with a tenebrous flapping of banners, like a man crying out at high noon—the city, sucked with me into the overflowing mirror of the evening, hauled out to sea in a spitting of embers, its monstrous breast under its columns of canvas cleaving the waters on a swell of noise and silence under the fog of living light and the burning bush of its flags.

CORTÈGE

———

Men 40–horses 8, this single regulatory inscription announced the mortuary bogie from afar—in waiting for more expressive marks of the glorious resurrection—not without having paraded in good order—only momentarily slowed by ascending the ramp—the first-class saloon cars where jade jewels sparkled on the fingers of pretty bridge players—busy passing the time that only materialized from one moment to the next—the one that the *dead man* wanted to devote to finally putting his cards on the table—the glance thrown through the car door on the moving and rainy expanse of an indifferent landscape.

THE *BONNE AUBERGE*

The guillotine of the black evening suit cuts the men off at the waist—the women, when kissed, attain the sharp vibration of crystal, then shatter, scattering adorable camellias of blood beneath the snow. With a noise of drays, the lord mayor's landau unloads one thing after another on the entrance steps; tea roses and heliotropes—the magistrate's mail coach: whip and wheels of mignonette green—the all-terrain vehicle of the morals police; hortensias and jonquils. And what to do now? The presentations finished, the couples having tied the knot, revolvers are fetched from pockets and the fete commences with a pigeon shoot aflame with broken glass. Like undertakers, the dress suits slip uneasily away two by two on leafy paths in the seedy dawn—a Berezina of fine glass debris is scattered over the deserted floors: the green plants; the Christmas trees of crackling snow and spun glass—several white souls reach the high regions of the skies in the form of delicate little angels—as light as an inconsequential instance in a metaphysical problem. One prefers not knowing what to think of an insouciance that disarms even the suspicions of justice.

JULIEN GRACQ

SURPRISE PARTIES AT THE HOUSE OF THE AUGUSTULES

———————

This morning the pavements are stairways where beautifully aligned cascades vaporize in a perspective of petrifying fountains. Not a breath of wind, but, on the boulevards, as far as the eye can see, the branches of the chestnut trees crack one by one with an audible sound of musket fire. From time to time some heraldic book bindings explode on the *bouquiniste* stalls along the Seine—giant seed pods burst open on the bars of cafes. Wooden faces everywhere; the day promises harsh weather; a dense hail of balls of laundry blue is reported at intervals on the Montagne Sainte-Geneviève. At the crack of dawn, crowds of postmen are at Saint-Julien-le-Pauvre, however, humble laundry workers coalesce at Saint-Nicholas-du-Chardonnet—the cannon is methodically fired every twenty seconds behind the altar of Saint-Germain-l'Auxerrois. It's unheard of, it scandalizes; at each detonation the archbishop makes pigeons fly out of his sleeve. Gazelles emerge in crowds from brothels and flock together on the municipal squares.

THE VALLEY OF JOSAPHAT

———

The landscape along the route, like fletches on the shaft of an arrow. I'm all alone. The empty inn where footsteps echo on the stone floor of floods. A bottle clinks, noises stick fast, time moves in crippled jerks, then forgets to move. Poor gestures are beaten down by the good bed of cool earth. Water tinkles solemnly. The glass is closed on the table like the lid on the bread bin. The flowing river of the mysterious route can be heard under a fog of cropped glebe land. To sleep, head on the table, in the center of the round of coolness.

On the room's streams of plaster milk, eyes move like the sunflower and the heliotrope, and are diluted in the inky stain of a black butterfly.

The Habitable Earth

———————

In every trajectory there's a vanishing point that splits time and stills the heartbeat; the one in which the firework, spent at the peak of its ascent, rests on a bed of air before bursting into flower—when the gymnast, midway between two trapezes, an interminable moment, presses against our diaphragm a nauseating emptiness—*a loss of speed* whereby the city we inhabit, and which day after day remakes for us, like those larvae of slowness that float on the shimmer of propeller blades, the single acceleration, the steering wheel thrown to the bottom of a maelstrom of mad orbits, becomes a ghost merely by allowing its immense body to be in a small way felt. The day that breaks on Paris is nothing like the planet's exultation, the orchestral sunrise in Beauce or Champagne; it's the blind reflux of an internal tide of blood—it's the appearance on a living face, at the surface of a closed life, of a sign of secret and gnawing weariness—the hour when life withdraws to its lowest ebb and when the dying expire—it's that poignant moment, that uncertain hour when the face *flies* from a beloved head on the pillow and, like a man walking on snow, the incomparable illumination of death points the way to an unknown mask.

This heart has beaten abundantly and now knows that so much beauty is mortal. There were mornings when, in the depth of the bed's mists, the first friendly banging of a shutter on the darkness was the reassuring nightlight that always burns in the window of someone dangerously ill—where the black streets were the doubtful intervals of a fleet of lofty prows at anchor, and where the reassuring echo of footsteps on asphalt couldn't conceal its revealed capacity for drowning. Today, in the acid air of the day breaking over Paris, something of the sailor's rough kick testing the deck of his ship still trails through empty streets, at the pace of the first walker—a taste of the daily bread melts in the mouth with the first lungful of air. The winged city rises up, shedding its cocoon of yellow fog, doubly moving in its strength and its fragility.

Whoever passes through Paris before daybreak passes uneasily by a numb building site in full swing, instantly summoning wild grass, massive machinery thrown brutally out of gear by the eye's sleep and the palm of man's hand, and already imperceptibly eroded, reduced to the panic state of landscape by I don't know what shroud of heaviness. A desert of walls as far as the eye can see, glistening roads and mirrors of clear water each morning propose to men the grueling task of making it all bloom, of clothing it and *blinding* it—like those demolished houses that are so precisely replaced by a palisade—with a seamless cloth of circuits, trajectories, and rumors. In these engineered scaffoldings, this labyrinth of shiny tracks, those piles of columns, the morning, like a withdrawing tide, reveals, to a troubling lack of response, this purely provocative aspect of an incomprehensible activity that, to a capital city, remains no less secret, no less essential than nudity is to a woman. That adventurous hour when Rastignac, from the heights of Père-Lachaise, answers the challenge, is in truth a forbidden hour. An entire people has secreted a carcass of monstrously proportionate size so as to lay out the robe of its millions of desires at arm's length from its full height. The sacrilegious eye that glides through the shivering nudity of a dawn in the streets of Paris catches something of the scandal of a naked seabed, of the disturbing snapshot of a wound not yet bleeding but that in a split second will overflow with blood. A hail of harsh caresses is ready to melt on that amorous vacancy; the city, feminized by the yawning labyrinth of a sleeping and uncovered belly, attaches the tensile energy of a tireless erethism to its secret grottoes, attracts the hungry and the solitary into the streets at the earliest hour and imbues the morning stroll with the absorbing and guilty character of possession.

Trembling on the extreme edge of nocturnal repose, there's a troubled intoxication in traversing that Baudelairean fringe of the "Parisian Dream" in which the city, redeemed from all servitude, is momentarily in lock step with the pure forms of space and time, where the tide of mists levels out along the smooth fault lines of the streets as in a plundered port, and where the city, swept along the course of its river, listens obsessively to the more attentive clocks sounding the hour, in that fascinating majesty that rebuilds a capital city in marble on the eve of an earthquake. With a disdainful heave the massive body has once more freed itself from everything that seeks to manage it, like a deity with empty blue eyes who, once more forsaken, lies down again to burden the horizon with a sheer weight. In one night, the inaccessible strangeness of the virgin forest returns to divorce man from the work of his hands. The rubbed eyes blink for a second on the frost of that petrifying necropolis, a helpful hand lays hold of the tools, the sun, free with a million energies, drives the ghost of an inhuman lucidity back to its mists, a tumultuous and assured blood boils in every vein, cushions a timbre of death, blurs inexorable perspectives, a deaf and blind, stupefying face is diluted in the day that dawns with the stars: for Paris, as for the biblical watchman, morning comes, and night too.

THE EXPLORER

There aren't many things I've experienced like those few lanes that yawned emptily at high noon, that went silently feral in an odor of sap and wild animal, their houses evacuated like a tidal wave under the foam of leaves. Like the plume of smoke from the explosion of a powder keg that flattens a town, great masses of stormy verdure rolled a somber sky over the wrecked roofs. The afternoon finds me before the high, blind wall of a park, straining my ears, as though detecting the rustle of leaves behind a door. In the open air, suddenly drenched by the wheeling sunlight as though by a brass band, my feet amorously arousing the secret slope of a hill as long as a cheek, every evening I came back down to the calm fields, my hands full like he who touches a woman, still pressing my forehead, eyes closed, as the heart fails and as one sleepwalks, in the fragrant dream and the void under the sun of this village leaning on the forest like a summer's afternoon on the balcony of its wild night.

MOSES

Eyes closed under the cool leaves of its privet shrubs, every afternoon the waterway carried me backward, like an Ophelia passing in her floral buoy, the soft enclosures slowly dissolving from her brow. Lying on the fundamental pillow, lower down than any other living creature, the trees' face fell on me like dew from a face bent over a sickbed, and putting the world softly afloat on my route like a cork, on a level with benign bovine muzzles, I was engaged to the resonant rings of bridges like gauze. Forgetting merged with a soft tisane of dead leaves in the black water of a forest's shadow on the river. Midday found me drifting in the sunlit expanse of vast glittering beaches, hands folded on heart, eyelids brilliant with languor, then the sumptuous rustling of reeds consumed the banks in a theatrical palisade of whispers, and, like a gown gently impeded by long-tailed stems, numb at the bottom of a green impasse, the gentle mesh of sunlit water that carried me like a womb, like someone gazing into the bottom of a pit, descended on me while resolving on a woman's face.

JULIEN GRACQ

ROOF GARDEN

There's a little green field on the rampart where eglantines, wallflowers, and the oats of the new day grow. Sometimes flowing like a yellow river, sometimes a skein under fingernails of air, sometimes the soft straw of blonde hair caught in a spinning wheel. With the evening, the thatched roofs are an altar of repose from which the town's charming plumes of smoke ascend like the corollas of a bombardment of festivals and silence, and with the women archers one sees the sky foaming with light clouds, and the countryside like a woman's breasts under the terrific heat. Stones are cleared from the field level with the emptiness and the roofs' carapace, and there are sheltered roads and peaceful paths through the grass, the stones, and the balsamic forest of nettles as far as the open platform where the sky over the sea of straw is a Mexican storm in which the air flows like oil in the mouth of a bronze cannon, and above the river the wild grass, like the shoulder of a horse, shivers for no reason.

INTIMACY

It's the hour when the vines and watering places return, the last hour. The wells are empty and the edge of the sheds are furred with turtledoves, a satin trim like red snow on the antiquated costumes that lean from the windows, under the necks of these birds of prey—foreign winds smelling of stubble and palm trees blow under porch doors—the carts pull on their hoods—it's cold here—smells provoke strange hungers under the lime trees and the bees, the kitchen tables sag under golden loaves of bread. Clamors and cries are heard very late from the crimson clearings off the empty house where the forgotten kettle sings on the calm embers. The sleep of the shutters on the lower chamber's aquarium gently refreshes the orange-flowered globe like a nocturnal egg in the hollow of the thatch, the hand that rattles the iron latch, the clock that splashes the anvil of silence. The marshland and the stable's hazy moonlight garland the floral night that ascends from the hollow cupboards, the aroma of caves and moldy shrouds, the rough burrow of the household bed, the mystical nudity of the spouse near the consoling lily of dark nights.

THE HIGH PLAINS OF SERTALEJO

For Jules Monnerot

I need only close my eyes to revive in memory the buoyancy of that season when we roamed, Orlando and myself, through the high plains of Sertalejo. I see again the clean-swept skies with the lustral clarity of a washed beach where clouds with pure outlines distributed the pearly whorls of seashells—the long green slopes swaying over the abysses, where the wind's fingers raked through the tall grass—the mountain lakes squeezed into the heart of the peaks' starry serrations like a puddle of nocturnal water in the hollow of a leaf. But, above all, the silence returns to haunt me with the fascination of a sustained chord in which the arabesques of the melody hasten to drown themselves as though in sleeping waters; a silence of high ground, of a devastated and smooth planet where there's nothing more on the ground to fray the shadows of the clouds, and where the sunlight explodes in a silent thunder of florescence.

We progressed in short stages, for in these plateaus a lead overcoat of weariness suddenly drops onto one's shoulders, and the rarefied air of the high altitudes fired up our hearts. We set out early in the morning when the air smelled of snow and stars and bit at the stomach—we rolled up our tents and cleaned the guns. For a while we made our way side by side, cheered by good morning talk, then we were split up by a narrowing of the trail, a rocky defile—words became fewer—and silence descended on our meager single file. Behind us, Jorge led the mules and, rasping dismally, our knees brushed against wastes of grass combed by the wind, like fording an endless stream.

We often crossed immense stretches of that dry and crackling grass, the color of straw, called the *pajonal*—and no desert of sand could convey the melancholy of that mummified and dead prairie, as though withered on the stalk by a mysterious ailment. Over that sea of straw the blue sky acquired a stormy hue, the crunching of our feet as we scythed through the dry stems put our teeth on edge with its small hail. The days of that leg of the journey were more silent than usual, and, absorbed by the ceaseless crackling of that frail sound of death, we went on in a vague malaise; it sometimes seemed to us that we were trampling on the scalp of the planet.

Perhaps nowhere else, it seemed to me, had the lines of nature arrived at such clarity, such lunar austerity. On the horizon every line was cruelly scoured by the acid air, sharpened, imbued with the cutting attack of a razor's edge on the eye. On that sad stubble not even the quiver of a trembling heat haze. We walked on, our breath shallow, eyes hurting, mouths parched, until the grass in front of us was spangled by a sudden trail and for a moment the crystal trap gripping our brows with its frost was shattered to pieces by a gunshot.

In crossing those high surfaces, we sometimes saw mountains coming toward us. Invariably it was the noble outlines of those great volcanoes that bore their crowns with the solitary majesty of shepherd kings on the high steppes of the Cordilleras. They usually declared themselves in the evening in the guise of a white cloud forming a cone anchored above the horizon in the purple mist. Morning suspended them on the horizon, glued to the sky by a nozzle of snow more incandescent than lava, tied to ground by nothing more than the pure line of a double filament of shadow, scarcely as yet distinguishable from the fog banks—similar on the high place of that immense table to the symmetrical and solemn gesture of hands displaying a holy relic. Then, as our feet forged through the grass, the apparition's drift on the flat horizon corresponded to the orb of a star, successively brightening all the corners of the sky—like a wound that enhances life—the skin of an angel rouged by the evening's crimson flares. The apparition melted away and then there was the deeper silence that the night sky acquires after the passage of a comet.

In the nights of those great grazing grounds, we felt the play of our lungs in our chests like an animal coming effortlessly awake, elastic and fine, with delicate

JULIEN GRACQ

epidermis. The evening wind in the high grass swept the last trace of moisture from the earth, offered it to the night sky in the coolness of a beach washed by cold seas. Instinctively we sought the site of a low hummock for our nighttime encampment; the flames, quickened by the wind, sent shimmering circles scudding far over the lustrous grass. We sat near the fire for a long time, surprised by that gleam on the horizon, above the black clumps of grass, that didn't want to die. The cold descended; Jorge passed over his poncho and went off toward the mules. Swaddled in the full length of his overcoat, he rocked bizarrely in the grass against the light on the surface, like a statue carried on a stretcher. Our vigil was prolonged by an exhilarating disquiet; on these plains pulsing like a sea the campsite weighed us down like a ship's anchor—we felt an urge to drift, as though unmooring a small boat on a moonlit night, and let ourselves glide among the outside shadows as in an open bed, fragrant and most secret. Orlando was asleep; I stole through the grass, smoothing the already frozen stems with the back of my hand, reaching the distant spot close to the mules where Jorge kept watch, and in the depths of that night I found two wide-open eyes, like hot soup and a fire at the end of a far-flung journey. The fire was dying; the glow of a few pink embers was the keenest point until morning on these high plains, as far as the distant horizon.

The migrant soul and the heart that surrenders itself to the pure journey find solace far from the houses of men, even if only for a brief season, a spreading of wings, a bloom of resurrection. On those nights when the cold took possession of the ground like a new realm, my heart fed on its strength. Stretched out at full length on this roof of the world, the palms of my hands open on the frozen grass, my eyes were diluted like ink in the clement depth of the night sky, my heaving chest surged like a tide in the infinite recession of space, my gaze burned in the pure air like the pure undirected gaze of a lookout, the cracked husk of stones delivered their living cold to my heart. In the heart of the dissolving night, all mooring ropes parted, all heaviness jettisoned, obedient to the breeze and borne on the water, I was a pure site of alliance and exchange. Half asleep already, in my overflowing contentment I squeezed the fingers of Jorge's hand in mine, in token of adieu and in token of a new advent.

The Siesta in Dutch Flanders

For Mme S. L.

————

On the eastern bank of the Scheldt, Dutch Flanders lays out a kind of cultivated desert reaching as far as the suburbs of Antwerp, a habitable margin where the lush and floral life of the Low Countries seems to make itself more discreet than elsewhere. No one goes there, and it's rarely traveled. The territory is poorly linked to Zeeland by some ferry lines that cross the Scheldt—the silhouette of a customs post very soon shows up along little paved roads on the Belgian side, decked out with flowers and asleep like a chalet in a health spa during the dead season, where the Dutch customs officers newly minted in their *surplus* Royal Air Force uniforms doze in a shaded room and stare with casual curiosity at the tourist who ventures into these outlying solitudes. You make leisurely small talk under the trees in a room as tiny as a small-town licensing office and guess that the customs officers know their world inside out, for whoever crosses the border here, Dutch day workers going to work in Bruges, or Belgian skippers of the Antwerp pilotage returning to Flushing, would as a rule hardly go much further. The frontier once passed, an intimate feeling very quickly insinuates itself into the traveler's spirit, informing us, even in the absence of any telltale signs, that somewhere *off the beaten track* lies ahead. You have to venture there at dusk, when the customs officers from the dayshift return to their nearby redbrick toy houses, pedaling straight ahead on their sit-up-and-beg bicycles, and, behind you, the vertical lines of Bruges's turrets and belfries, similar on these low plains to the distant *skyline* of an American city, darken into blue at the crenels of rows of poplars. In running northward, the empty roads seem little by little to bleed away, diverging and diminishing into smaller paths that flee indefinitely behind their lines of trees through the verdant desert. Roofs no longer jut up behind the masses of trees, and no lights are still shining. A scent of grass and succulent leaves fills the evening, as immersive as the smell of a wet animal; the herds resting in the distance of the great meadows, already misted over, seem caught in the frozen eddies of the high grass as though in the lime of a slushy ice field; you get the impression that the life petrified in that savage verdure is gradually going numb, to terminate a little further on, behind that curtain of poplars. In the cool of the evening, it's good to ride along these muffled and leafy roads that very soon leave you wondering whether they lead anywhere at all, zigzagging on the crest of dikes between the titanic caissons of polders made equal by the twilight, and which, in their monotonous symmetry, succeed each other like immense ferries, heavily decant-ing water that's greasy under its thick nap of green foam. Here, the foliage loses the waywardly variable quality to be found in hill country; rather it *rises* on the flat-bot-tomed squares of this enormous checkerboard—uni-form, greedy, engulfing, sprawling—like the level of the sea in a tidal basin, or rather like a flooded paddy field where the densely-woven carpet of green shoots, com-peting in speed with the water, seems to lift itself up like a floating crust. No stitching on this green gown—no rents in this plush and universal lining; ripe grass seeps up from the uneven paving of the roads, and even the top of the dikes is a silent and undulating carpet where the isolated track of a cyclist closes up again like fur stroked by a finger. The road carries on, however, narrower and more uneven—a final curve and a steep little path climbs a dike that hid the view; just at present the green lepro-sy hasn't made any further inroads and you can see the broad and gray Scheldt which, at low tide, regretfully exposes to the bite of its adversary's teeth the big, vul-nerable pools of the naked water of its mudflats that the clutching grass hooks onto. The smoke of cargos sailing toward Antwerp trails with lazy insolence between the hostile breastplates of those riverbanks that wallow in a heavy and agricultural lethargy—having sped back down nothing more can be seen; however you're soon made aware of the nearness of the sea by the keener breath that washes over these broad and airy prospects, by the rapidly changing skies that send the shadows of clouds flitting over the lakes of grass, and the remindful seabirds whose raucous swarms whirl briefly above the poplars before returning to the mudflats for the night. The point of view shifts; on that ocean silted with fields the dense sails of the poplars fleetingly resume for the informed eye the noble perspective of ships of the line under their canvas towers, just like the old Dutch history paintings on the ground floor of the Rijksmuseum.

All this territory, very recently diked, has emerged from water, evidently, in the explosion of florescence that follows a deluge. However, the emptiness and silence of these exuberant landscapes are intriguing. You might say that life is intimidated by this new and stiff material divided into over-regular and over-ample strips, precarious in its hold on these alien cyclopean segments. Gripping the dikes, it proceeds like an insect following the seams of the floor, cautiously invading by way of the strips that prefabricated Eden of verdure whose austere and distended geometry leaves it disoriented; one would say that a kind of *agoraphobia* instinctively pushes it back toward the shaded borders of the big grass seedbeds. There are no towns and scarcely any villages. Man is discouraged from preferring one place to another on the seamless juxtaposition of this agricultural tiling; it first takes firm hold in the angles, in the way that spiderwebs colonize a new house. Occasionally a tiny village leans into the acute angle of two dikes; the roofs of toy cottages are

JULIEN GRACQ

exactly flush with the level of the dike; you hardly see the village before coming upon it from above; the eye swoops down onto the flowering window borders and the small, tiled, frighteningly spotless rooms, and you can see the start of the rigid little guillotine stairs. No one to be seen, the little gardens are empty, the village is so tiny it could be held in the palm of the hand, warming itself there, quiet as a mouse, cradled in the pale sunlight, its little display of domestic *farniente* pleasing to the eye, like the crew's hammocks under the open hatches of the foredeck. Opulence has taken refuge in the big, new, and well-ordered farms with their gleaming bricks; sometimes after zigzagging over the right angles of these open and yet so apparently *destined* squares until overcome by tiredness, you suddenly discover one of them from the top of a dike and feel an intimate little shudder in noting that this time the honeycomb is inhabited, but no path radiates out from it, the immaculate green carpet is unmarked by any surrounding abrasion; none of those fine lines woven by the long cultivation of fields fasten it to the countryside—it's simply placed there, an immaculate and oddly abstract signifier of occupation rather than presence, indifferent and movable, like a piece on a chessboard square. There's no coming or going around the mute buildings, and not even a cock crowing in the yard; under their roofs that ride the gables all the way to the ground, like a horseman's forked legs distended by an enormous belly, they have the weighty rumination of a *dolphin* up to its nostrils in plankton or of a herd sprawled out in the afternoon of the Prairie; even their names: Baarn, Graauw, Saaftingen, seem to yawn on the central double vowel that drawls like a lazy and bucolic mooing. However, you let yourself picture these plump, well-to-do farms, their soft sides stuffed with harvested crops, as leading a charmed life—the charm of being forgotten and more subtly interred behind the disconcerting anonymity of their similar buildings; perhaps nowhere else in the world are you able to feel yourself living indistinguishably *anywhere*—anywhere lost in the savannah's hospitable tract, in the landscaped breadth of grassland, walled in the heart of the directionless labyrinth of a screen of poplars folded back on itself and replicated a thousandfold. The desert has its perspectives that engulf the imagination, the forest has the hidden life of its sounds and shadows—here, the intimate feeling of being lost, without fret or fever, becomes subtler and more absorbing. You can wander for hours from one square to another of that immense game of snakes and ladders, in the obsessive rustling of poplars and the smell of crushed grass, the view never extends further than the next dike and the next curtain of trees; no one sees from the flat bottom of each of the combs, and no one is seen; a similar dike stretches out behind the first dike, and beyond the screen of trees yet another screen of poplars. No angst in this impeccable and manicured labyrinth with the rich green of an English lawn; people are there, close at hand, and the roads are navigable; a sign is all that's needed, but what's lacking is the desire to make that sign, and, caught in the obsessive maze of these vegetal chambers, you swiftly realize how redundant would be the need to steer for any rallying point. The idea suddenly occurs that you could lay yourself down here, no longer thinking of anything, wrapped in the aroma and the thick overcoat of fresh leaves, face washed by the light breeze, the perpetual soft rustle of the poplars in your ears familiarizing you with the sound of plenitude itself. It's only in this immense volume of calm that a certain *basis*, essential to life, is precipitated. Suddenly everything is very far away, the contours of every thought dissolve into the green mist, the final chamber of the labyrinth opens onto an intimate disposition of the soul into which you hesitate to look; it's the human plant that's called on to make it unfold, the mysterious flower sheltered there, in an intoxicated acquiescence to the deep spirits of Indifference. You succumb at full length, on the grass. Thought abandons its tedious observation posts and dismantles its network of useless aerials; it flows back from all sides to the limit point of pure consciousness of being; the frontiers of the body are no more than a light perspiration with no other seeming purpose than to refresh us as we correspondingly evaporate, dissolving to nothingness an excess of rising sap, in the thick vegetal secretion, the apoplexy of that green nature and that clay with its intimate memories of the sea. The world flows back on us, compact in the withdrawal of the sharp-edged question marks that lacerate it; the body that presses down the still soft soil under the grass seems to be made for nothing other than imparting to the greedy breathing that lifts it the feeling of a still unknown functional liberty; you could say that the earth's pores open wider here than elsewhere. No more horizon but rather the immaterial opacity of a tulle veil that like a mosquito net brings toward this waking sleep an immoderate orgy of inattention; the contraction of that delicate bubble of transparency traps all round us, unmutilated, an undifferentiated morsel of sufficient nature; nothing outside the rustle of cool grass under the palms of the hand, the glitter against the sky of aspen leaves that seem to give a sharper edge to immobility, and in this *middle* in which all pressures are made equal and annulled, an unanchored bottle imp that floats ad nauseam between grass and clouds. This moment, and this narrow bit of ground, holds in us its totality and its sufficiency—there's no longer an elsewhere—there never has been anywhere else—all things are in perfect communion in the permeable; you feel yourself here, on the magnetic margins of absorption, a droplet among droplets, expressed a moment before coming home from the earth's soft sponge.

JULIEN GRACQ

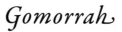

Gomorrah

In those days—the longest of the year—great battle tanks lay in wait throughout the Cinglais thickets elbow to elbow with the wild forest sows, the volley of their guns charcoaled against the setting sun of Louis XIII chateaus. The light was out of step with the time of day— the shadow of the bushes across the road more delectable than cool water on account of the bright metal flies and the commotion in the bad hornet's nest sky. It was a pleasure to be pressing on in the open air; the open roads, the folding-doors—the flying column under the plane trees on the lawn of sour grass in the evacuated manor house, away from the stifling city. A thunderstorm splashed big drops on the dishes; through open double windows the children's camp beds could be seen under the family portraits, in a salon better deployed than a cavalry charge. The Orne flowed—very slowly—out front among the privets and flowering fields filled with rushes. The slacking of life's grip pleased me, and that you made your bed in dim houses as though in the depths of a dark wood.

When I arrived at the May hillside, the slope was half in shadow and half sunlit; the birds sang less loudly; ahead of me on the very white road was a young woman I knew; I joined her. I learned that she was also stopping at Jaur, and that as guests we were to sleep in the same house. We walked on. The countryside was a delight; those slopes that climbed between the forests, the coolness of the leaves and the damp clay verges where puddles persist right into the heart of summer. We sometimes talked and sometimes fell silent. There were clusters of black pines planted where the roads forked, or an occasional wayside cross—but best of all was a summer evening that, thanks to *l'heure allemande*, kept the fields awake supernaturally late, like harvest time. At Thury I stopped for supper at the inn; the low sun still flamed on the windowpanes and the copper of the cupboards—between courses I looked up at the empty road that flowed on from the open door, limpid and pure, like a river that one diverts through one's garden. I set off again, lit up by the song of a bottle of wine like a lantern by its candle. Behind me, one after another, the sirens unleashed their diminuendo on the city marked out for fire. Never again would there be any cause for concern. Blanched by the moon, the road ahead was so delicately illuminated that you could distinguish the young blades of grass between the fine gravel on the verges. The Jaur belfry, at a few stones' throw, flanked the path in the night marked by a tender sign, like a white gown in the shadow of a garden—the road headed South, a sandy surface between the round tents of the apple tree in the open night, and I sang because I was expected.

Aubrac

It takes very little to live here. From this balcony, where the mountain leans at that time of day when the sun is at its yellowest, there's nothing left to choose except the bench on the right where the grass darkens to black under the chestnut trees, the distant Viadène on the left, already bright blue. Halfway down the slope, the day draws breath. From that ample and covered gallery where the pink gravel road slips by above the partridge-gray Causse, one can see long shadows ripen low down in the plum-colored light. Everything recommends a pause for rest at this still temperate wayside shelter on tilting ground, to inhale the luxuriant air of the water-sprinkled park, the day that garners itself in rays of honey and the warmth of amber, until the eye, surfeited, returns to the pink road that climbs under the sun before turning into the shadows of a pine wood, and that your hand already cools with the evening—your hand through which the clearer sounds of the mountain stream filter, your hand that gives me the autumn crocuses.

We will climb higher. There, higher than all the trees, where the basalt-coated earth lifts and smooths out an immensely empty palm in the blue air, at the coldest time of day when your naked feet will sink into the breathing fur, when your hair will shake out the smell of wild hay in the wind riddled with stars, while we walk as though on waves over ground as naked as a mare toward the lighthouse of black lava.

TRANSLATOR'S AFTERWORD
THE SIESTA

In 1929, the Belgian surrealist journal *Variétés* published a surrealist map of the world. In this version, Ireland remains in place, but Britain, Spain, Portugal, Italy and the Low Countries have vanished, along with the United States (with the exception of an oversized Alaska). Russia is massive. France, for its part, is reduced to a single location, namely Paris.[1] Gracq, if he saw this, would have been sardonically amused. Geography was, for him, a lifelong passion; he studied it at the École normale supérieure, and, while teaching at Caen University in the 1940s, he researched a thesis on the regional geography of Lower Normandy. From 1947 until his retirement in 1970 he taught geography and history at the Lycée Claude-Bernard, Paris. He traveled in France and, whenever the opportunity arose, abroad, visiting a variety of European destinations. After retirement there were further travels, notably, in 1970, to various locations in the United States (in one of which he made the acquaintance of August Derleth). Correspondingly, travel and place play an important part in Gracq's oeuvre—an increasingly central one from *A Balcony in the Forest* onward; his writing of landscape and topography always carries particular conviction.

Great Liberty, full of geographical place names and foreign sites, is bookended by two major texts, both focused on topography; "To Galvanize Urbanism" provides the Parisian incipit, while at the far end of the volume we find "The Siesta in Dutch Flanders." These texts also provide *Great Liberty* with an overall orientation: what starts as a castigation of urban sclerosis eventually culminates in "The Siesta" as a radiant union with nature.

"The Siesta in Dutch Flanders," like certain other texts added to the 1958 edition, also evidences a partial retreat from the avant-garde poetics of the 1946 edition. This should not be seen as a rejection of surrealism; "Paris at Dawn," the first in order of the 1958 inclusions, goes some way toward reprising the hallucinated visions and saturated prose of "To Galvanize Urbanism." Shorter entries, "The Explorer," "Moses," "Roof Garden," and "Intimacy," also sustain the associative freedoms of the earlier prose poems, although in a more gently pastoral mode. Where the volume's four final texts are concerned, however—"The High Plains of Sertalejo," "The Siesta in Dutch Flanders," "Gomorrah," and "Aubrac"— surrealism is less a birth mother than a benevolent godparent. It might be tempting to detach these texts from the rest of *Great Liberty* and see them as operating on a different level, more "readerly" than "writerly," to use Barthes's distinction.[2] This would be a mistake: "The Siesta in Dutch Flanders," in its evocation of "a still unknown functional liberty," both continues and completes the overall thematic itinerary of *Great Liberty*; the poetic vision that animates the volume finds its fullest expression in this text.

The landscape of the polders—low-lying land reclaimed from the sea and enclosed by square dikes—first left its mark on Gracq during his brief Dutch and Belgian military sorties in 1940. He returned to Holland in the summer of 1948, then revisited Belgium in the winter of 1949, taking advantage of an invitation to an Antwerp conference extended by the Belgian writer Suzanne Lilar, to whom "The Siesta" is dedicated. In 1950 he wrote to her, "I'm pleased to offer you this little text. . . . It concerns a territory close to you, I don't know how well I understand it, but it's ended up becoming a singular site of convergence for me. I used to dream so much of Lohengrin's swan and Elsa de Brabant, then the war led me to these banks of the Scheldt . . . —Finally, it's a place I'm very sensitive to. The three days spent there in 1940 . . . left me with a persistent, strange impression."[3] The letter alerts us to the overtones of legend in the text, and also to a faint echo of war. In writing "The Siesta," Gracq returned to his earlier account of the polders in the still unpublished *Manuscrits de guerre*, borrowing, here and there, an image, a phrase, a sentence (the reference, early in the text, to surplus Royal Air Force uniforms worn by the customs officers also reminds us of the recent hostilities).

Gracq's "strange impression" is well conveyed. Along with "Aubrac," "The Siesta" presents an evolved version of a distinctively Gracqian genre of geographical and topographical surrealism that is realized throughout *Great Liberty*. The writer draws directly on his travels and memories, but at no point does he use the first-person singular, while a plural "we" occurs only once near the beginning and twice near the end. Otherwise, the narrative voice is impersonal, displaced onto "the traveler" and "one" ("on," translated here as "you"); impressions and perceptions are freed from the self-awareness that ballasts subjectivity. Until the conclusion, there is none of the bodily awareness that grounds the experience of travel; this is a journey that proceeds flowingly and effortlessly, as though in a dream.

Impersonalization rubs shoulders with depersonalization. Following the brief early encounter with the customs personnel the traveler never meets another soul; few other Gracq narratives are so devoid of human presence. The story begins on a borderline, namely the river Scheldt that separates Holland from Flanders, and proceeds by way of an encounter with the threshold guardians—the local customs officers. Leaving the known world (Bruges) behind him, the traveler ventures into a debatable land: "somewhere *off the beaten track* lies ahead. You have to venture there at dusk . . ." (Gracq's emphasis). As in "The Ross Barrier" and "Sertalejo," the narrator ventures into an uncannily defamiliarized region devoid of human presence, but only in "The Siesta" does he do so under conditions of complete solitude.

The imagined landscapes of the Antarctic and the Andes are romantically sublime, but there's nothing romantic about the Mondrian-like landscape that the traveler now encounters. This is an engineered territory, an "enormous checkerboard" with "agricultural tiling." The images anticipate one of Alain Robbe-Grillet's motifs (". . . the black and white tiles on the floor . . . The large squares were of a uniform gray"[4]). Gracq, writing later, was critical of the Nouveau Roman school, with Robbe-Grillet as a particular bête noire; in "The Siesta," however, he comes dangerously close to preempting Robbe-Grillet's investment in closely observed surfaces at the expense of subjective depths. Gracq's disembodied traveler flattens the landscape, comparing it with paintings in the Rijksmuseum, and also a game of snakes and ladders. The prospect in view is specifically alien: "Life is intimidated, its hold on these alien cyclopean segments precarious." The polders are experienced as impersonally estranging. Meanwhile we have lost track of time—is it night or day? What exactly is the mode of transport—car, bicycle, on foot? Where exactly are we on the map? None of these questions are answered, an indetermination that seems to contrast with the geometrical precision of the polders, but in fact corresponds to the traveler's ultimate experience of them as a labyrinth.

In *La Forme d'une ville* (*The Form of a City*), Gracq remarks on "the prestige of miniaturization."[5] When human habitations come into view in "The Siesta" they are miniaturized and eerily empty: "The roofs of toy cottages are exactly flush with the level of the dike. . . . No one in sight, the little gardens are empty, the village is so tiny it could be held in the palm of the hand." In his study *The Uncanny*, Nicholas Royle notes that "there has to be a sense of home and homeliness in order within and beyond which to think the unhomely."[6] The uncanniness of the polder dwellings is physically felt as a "shudder" by the traveler as he proceeds,

> An intimate little shudder in noting that this time the honeycomb cell is inhabited, but no path radiates out from it, the immaculate green carpet is unmarked by any surrounding abrasion; none of those fine lines woven by the long cultivation of fields fasten it to the countryside—it's simply placed there, an immaculate and oddly abstract signifier of occupation rather than presence, indifferent and movable, like a piece on a chessboard square.

Here, the traveler is surveying an enchanted realm, a domain of the Sleeping Beauty,[7] but one that is translated into the rigidly compartmentalized terms of a Louis XIV garden.

A seemingly endless proliferation of tracts, paths, and trees is geometrically ordered but now experienced as a "directionless labyrinth" in which the traveler loses himself. But this is a prison that doesn't imprison—the labyrinth is an open space, not a closed one, and loss of direction is accepted tranquilly, even happily: "no angst in this impeccable and manicured labyrinth." With the realization that there is no central "rallying point," the traveler paradoxically arrives at its center—"the final chamber of the labyrinth opens."

According to the Freudian anthropologist Géza Róheim, "The ritual of the labyrinth originates in the process of going to sleep":[8] the deceptive banality of the text's title is enacted as the sudden notion of enjoying a snooze: "you could stretch yourself out here, thinking of nothing else . . . you succumb, at full length on the grass." With this initiative, the narrative is transformed: what has been an exclusively outward focus now becomes an inward, subjective one. Embedded in greenery, the traveler at last acquires a tactile awareness of his own body.

The visionary reverie that follows can be read in part as a reply to the existentialist humanism that replaced surrealism in the French cultural mainstream after 1939.[9] At the conclusion of Camus's *L'Étranger* (*The Outsider*, 1942), Meursault, imprisoned in his condemned cell, and following a furious confrontation with a priest, achieves a moment of final realization: "As though that great anger had purged me of wrong, emptied out all hope, in that night filled with signs and stars I opened myself for the first time to the world's tender indifference."[10] In the paper he gave in

Antwerp in 1949, Gracq, who respected Camus, nevertheless singled out *L'Étranger* for attack: "as for Camus, the image he gives of man in *L'Étranger*, victim of the absurd, separated from himself, is properly speaking one of total alienation and hopelessness."[11] The "final chamber" of Gracq's verdant labyrinth both parallels and replies to Meursault's prison cell. When he asserted in 1947 that André Breton refused to accept life understood as jail time and laid claim to a "hope beyond all hope," Gracq also spoke for himself.[12] It's likely, then, that he had in mind the imprisoned Meursault's fatalistic acceptance in envisioning in "The Siesta" an antithetically affirmative version of indifference—*l'Indifférence*:

> the final chamber of the labyrinth opens onto an intimate disposition of the soul into which you hesitate to look; it's the human plant that's called on to make it unfold, the mysterious flower sheltered there, in an intoxicated acquiescence to the deep spirits of Indifference.[13]

The intriguing expression "the human plant" suggests a vital organic symbiosis that opposes the negatively encroaching mineralization of "Truro." The phrase, Boie comments, "is the first appearance in Gracq of a term that will be decisive in defining his conception of poetry; the trustful, wonderstruck feeling of a presence in the world whereby his oeuvre opposes all the literature of 'exclusion.'"[14] She refers us to Gracq's 1960 lecture, "Pourquoi la littérature respire mal" (Why literature can't breathe):

> in reading those stifling novels [Sartre to Robbe-Grillet] from which the open air and the outside world are excluded . . . what strikes me is a deliberate and systematic exclusion.

> Exclusion of that kind of marriage . . . that is sealed each day and each minute between man and the world that carries him, and is the foundation of what, for my part, I've called *the human plant*.[15]

An implicitly Sartrean nausea is invoked when, in "Written on Water," Gracq refers to "my body like a livid goatskin bottle, decaying like everything possessing a stomach." In "The Siesta" we arrive at a diametrically opposed awareness:

> The frontiers of the body are no more than a light perspiration with no other seeming purpose than to refresh us as we correspondingly evaporate, dissolving to nothingness an excess of rising sap, in the thick vegetal secretion, the apoplexy of that green nature and that clay with its intimate memories of the sea.

This account of an intimately permeable communion, hinting at an ecological Eros, glows through the translucent skin of the text like a 100-watt light bulb held behind it. Here again there is an implicit opposition to "the literature of exclusion": "What Robbe-Grillet writes and rewrites . . . is at bottom another *Étranger*, a different *Étranger* from that of Camus insofar as the outside world takes the place of the hero as an obdurate, impenetrable opacity."[16]

In marking the culmination of his journey by lying down and going to sleep, the traveler simultaneously awakens to a visionary awareness, one that clarifies and develops the "new advent" that concludes "The High Plains of Sertalejo." In the "First Surrealist Manifesto," Breton states, "I believe in the future resolution of those two states—outwardly so contradictory—that are dream and reality, into a sort of absolute reality, a *surreality*."[17] This, evidently, made an impression on Gracq; he quotes it twice in immediately succeeding pages of *André Breton*.[18] The *coincidentia oppositorum* of the "waking sleep" ("ce sommeil éveillé") acquires *surreality* as its ultimate form. Surrealism persists here not as an avant-garde movement that has passed its sell-by date, but as a counter-existential quest, the "changing, fleeting silhouette in quest of the great adventure, like those of the knights errant who disappeared behind the thrust of their lance . . . a *supernatural* quest."[19] The image, in the conclusion of *André Breton*, is provided by Dürer,[20] but also refers back to Gracq's discussion, earlier in the book, of the company of surrealists as a "closed order . . . much closer, by virtue of its particularly exclusive contours, to the Round Table or the knightly quest for the Grail."[21] Though invited by Breton, Gracq chose not to join that company. Nevertheless, the conclusion of "The Siesta" can be read as the quester's encounter, following a solitary rite of passage, with the object of the quest. Victor Turner summarizes the rite:

> All rites of passage or "transitions" are marked by three phases: separation, margin (or limen or "threshold" in Latin), and aggregation. The first phase of separation comprises the detachment of the individual . . . from an earlier fixed point. . . . During the intervening "liminal" period, the characteristics of the ritual subject are ambiguous; he passes through a cultural realm that has few or none of the attributes of the past or coming state. In the third phase (reaggregation or reincorporation), the passage is consummated.[22]

From this we can infer the ritual nature of the Flanders journey, and in so doing absolve it from any anticipation of the *chosisme* of Robbe-Grillet. The river Scheldt, a line of separation, is succeeded by a pilgrimage or quest in which past and future, individual self-hood and self-determination, are suspended. This is the necessary prelude to the consummation that occurs in the heart of the labyrinth. Gracq would have recognized Turner's term "reincorporation," which is rooted in the Latin for embodiment; returned to his body, the traveler is reincorporated with the world, enabling "that kind of marriage . . . that is sealed each day and each minute between man and the world that carries him."

In the final 1966 edition of *Great Liberty*, Gracq added one further, concluding text, namely "Aubrac," an evocation of the Massif Central. In *Carnets du grand chemin* (Highway notebooks, 1992), he commented on the powerful attraction that this territory held for him:

> An attraction that isn't violent but that's difficult to resist brings me, year after year, again and again, back to the high naked surfaces—basalt or chalk—at the center and the south of the Massif: Aubrac, Cézallier, the planezes,[23] the Causses. Everything that remains of the integrally exotic in the French countryside seems to me to be quartered there. . . . Austere, sacramental tonsures in our continual shaggy arborescence, images of an almost spiritual excoriation of the landscape that for the walker indissolubly melds the feeling of altitude with the feeling of elevation.[24]

TRANSLATOR'S AFTERWORD

The movement from "Venice," one of *Great Liberty*'s early texts, to "Aubrac" at its conclusion can be seen as a poetic journey through a *terra incognita*, completed by an eventual homecoming to the strangeness, spirituality, and surreality of one's own native ground.

NOTES

1. The map is reproduced in Waldberg, *Surrealism*, 24.

2. "Roland Barthes in his book *S/Z* ... used the terms *lisible* ("readerly") and *scriptible* ("writerly") to distinguish, respectively, between texts that are straightforward and demand no special effort to understand and those whose meaning is not immediately evident and demand some effort on the part of the reader" ("Readerly and Writerly," *Encyclopedia Britannica*, https://www.britannica.com/art/readerly).

3. *OC* 1, 1237.

4. Robbe-Grillet, *The Voyeur*, trans. Richard Howard (London: John Calder, 1959), 59. The checkerboard image occurs elsewhere in Robbe-Grillet, for example in the short text, "The Dressmaker's Dummy," in *Snapshots*: "a waxy oilcloth patterned in red and gray squares."

5. In *OC* 2, 780.

6. Royle, *The Uncanny* (Manchester: Manchester University Press, 2003), 25.

7. Cf. *Un balcon en forêt*: "This emptiness ... was strange, improbable, somewhat magical: an alley in the castle of the Sleeping Beauty." *OC* 2, 107.

8. Róheim, *The Gates of Dream* (New York: International Universities Press, 1969), 260.

9. In an essay-length entry on Gracq in *The International Encyclopedia of Surrealism* (ed. Michael Richardson et al.), Atsuko Nagaï tells us that "In *What is Literature* published in 1947, Sartre disparaged Breton whom he saw as belonging to a prewar generation that was no longer relevant (. . .). Gracq defended Breton against these reproaches" (London: Bloomsbury, 2019) vol. 2, 336.

10. Camus, *Oeuvres complètes: Theatre, récits, nouvelles* (Paris: Gallimard, Bibliothèque de la Pléiade, 1962), 1209.

11. "Le Surréalisme et la littérature contemporaine," *OC* I, 1029.

12. See *André Breton*, *OC* I, 471.

13. The French term *Indifférence* (capitalized by Gracq) is literally translated as "indifference"; however, in contrast with the English, it's more closely akin (via the shared Latin root *indifferentia*) to *indifférencié*—"undifferentiated." In the French text there is arguably a degree of implied feedback between "[les] esprits profondes de l'Indifférence" and the subsequent reference to "un morceau indifférencié de la nature" ("an undifferentiated morsel of nature"), thus further muting any negative connotations of "indifferent."

14. In *OC* I, 1237–1238.

15. *OC* I, 878–879.

16. *OC* I, 875–876.

17. In Waldberg, *Surrealism* (trans. Waldberg), 70.

18. *OC* I, 440–441.

19. *André Breton*, *OC* I, 514.

20. Gracq refers specifically to Dürer's engraving *Knight, Death, and the Devil*.

21. *OC* 1, 414.

22. Victor Turner, "Liminality and Community," in J. C. Alexander and S. Seidelman, eds., *Culture and Society: Contemporary Debates* (Cambridge: Cambridge University Press, 1992), 47.

23. "Planeze" is a technical geographical term: "Sloping triangular facet on the flank of a volcano, underlain and protected by lava" (Oxford Reference, https://www.oxfordreference.com/view/10.1093/oi/authority.20110803100033021).

24. *OC* 2, 992.

NOTES ON THE TEXTS

TO GALVANIZE URBANISM

THE INEVITABLE *REMORA*: a slender marine fish that attaches itself to large fish by means of a sucker on top of the head. It generally feeds on the host's external parasites.

THE PENETRATING BELL OF A *REAL* COW: "This collage effect derives from an actual collage, . . . ; the *Revue surréaliste* 12 (Dec. 1929) published on p. 46 an unsigned representation of the facade of the Palais Garnier in front of which a field of cows and a pond replaced the Place de l'Opéra" (Boie, in *OC* 1, 1225).

IT'S SAINT-NAZAIRE I WANT TO TALK ABOUT: a port city in Brittany, "a stopping point on Gracq's holiday agenda throughout his youth" (Boie, in *OC* 1, 1225).

THE WHITENESS OF LEGENDARY SWANS: "my fanatical fondness for *Lohengrin* finally takes me to the bank of the Scheldt, looking out for the appearance of the swan" (*Manuscrits de guerre*, 52).

THE MILD AND LUMINOUS RIVER OF TOURAINE: i.e., the Loire.

WELLS'S GIANT TRIPODS FROM MARS: See the introduction for a discussion of the *War of the Worlds* reference.

ONE OF THOSE *ODD IDEAS*: Following Poe and André Breton, Gracq made a habit of italicizing certain terms. "With reference to italics in Breton, Gracq speaks of 'an increasing valorization' of meaning that the italic can also confer on the word 'to magically multiply its power'" (Cécile Narjoux, "Une énergique du mot; Italique et guillemets dans *Un balcon en forêt*," *Poétique* 4, no. 152 (2007): 479–505, https://www.cairn.info/revue-poetique-2007-4-page-479 .html). There's a debt to symbolism as much as to surrealism in Gracq's view of "le mot"—the word. In a 1987 review of André Hardellet's *Les Chasseurs*, he remarks that language is poetically enriched by "glossary fragments of a magical kind where the words recover what's natural and consubstantial with them, the sovereign liberty to evoke rather than signify" (*OC* 2, 1188). See the introduction for his discussion in *André Breton* of word versus syntax. The continuity between the remarks on Breton (1947) and Hardellet (1987) underlines the cohesion of the Gracquian poetics that inform *Great Liberty*.

. . . HOISTED THE ENORMOUS HULL OF THE LINER "NORMANDY" BETWEEN ITS BLOCKS: "At Saint-Nazaire a fifteen-year-old Julien Gracq witnesses the launch of the *Île-de-France* and, between

1930 and 1932, the construction of the *Normandie*. These sights precipitated two images; that of the cathedral (the *Normandie* 313 meters long and 39 meters high dominates the city's buildings), and that of the launch. . . . The image of the ship, first immobile on its cradle, then sliding into the sea, obeys a desire to liberate the world from its weight, to express the secret vibration, the promises of movement harbored by things apparently condemned to immobility" (Boie, in *OC* 1, 1226).

LIKE THE MASTLESS BARGE OF THE POET UNDER HIS MILD, AD-VENTUROUS SKY: see Baudelaire's "Les sept vieillards"—"vieille gabarre/ Sans mâts" ("an old barge/ Without masts . . .").

BUT DOES IT STILL EXIST, THIS SAINT-NAZAIRE OF WHICH I DREAM IN THE DEPTH OF MY ROOM, IT AND SO MANY OTHERS?: see the introduction, note 24. Boie reads this question as being prompted by the Allied bombing of Saint-Nazaire.

IT'S TO THIS MYTH: "Amphion became a great singer and musician after his lover Hermes taught him to play and gave him a golden lyre. Zethus [Amphion's brother] became a hunter and herdsman. . . . Amphion and Zethus built the fortifications of Thebes. . . . While Zethus struggled to carry his stones, Amphion played his lyre and his stones followed after him and gently glided into place" (Wikipedia: https://en.wikipedia.org/wiki/Amphion_and_Zethus).

AFTER ALL, APPEARANCES ARE NOTHING TO THE DEVIL AND, LAME AS HE SEEMINGLY IS, LIKE JUSTICE, HE'LL NEVER BE FINISHED WITH BLOWING UP ROOFS: Three points to note here:

1. "appearances are nothing to the devil": Gracq's French text reads, "Le diable . . . n'y perd rien," literally "the devil loses nothing," but this would be an incorrect translation; the phrase is a colloquial expression with no convenient English equivalent; depending on context, it can be understood as "the situation isn't how it might appear" or "appearances are deceptive." Gracq, however, plays on an untranslatable double meaning; he reintroduces the literal devil by way of referencing Lesage's eighteenth-century picaresque fantasy *Le diable boiteux* (The lame devil). My translation, "appearances are nothing to the devil," is a makeshift expedient.

2. "Like justice": "here Gracq allies a popular image—that of justice (the expression 'justice follows crime with a lame foot') with a literary reminiscence, that of Lesage's *Diable boiteux*" (Boie, in *OC* 1, 1227).

3. "He'll never be finished with blowing up roofs": see the introduction for a discussion of this phrase.

VENICE

I RANG AT THE GATES OF THE PALAZZO MARTINENGO: "no less than three palazzos exist that bear the name commemorating the ancient Venetian family. But here, as in so many other passages, reverie takes hold of a fragment of reality in order to assimilate it into the poetic imaginary" (Boie, in *OC* 1, 1227).

A FEW MINUTES MORE AND THE DUNES SOUNDING THE RETREAT: Urban Venice has no directly available beaches. The Lido, the nearest beach, has to be reached by vaporetto, and its sand dunes are well to the south. There would appear to be a hallucinatory leakage of Breton imagery into the scene as described. In *A Dark Stranger*, Gérard and Christel are discussing Venice while strolling on a golf course behind a Breton beach: "All Venice was in a little square of black water, furiously shining and frizzling under the sun with a tireless lapping of water. The same thing here, I love nothing more than those long, trimmed lawns behind the dunes, from whence you turn your shoulders to the sea, but with the massive noise of the sea close at hand" (*OC* 1, 109). Like a dream version of Gérard's remark, the Palazzo Martinengo scene seems to involve a superimposed image of a Breton seashore, creating the effect of a double exposure. In private communication, Clive Scott remarks that "part of Gracq's poetry is the way in which elements from different fields/locations redistribute themselves in new landscapes and dynamic interactions."

DURING THE ORCHESTRA'S MOONLIGHT INTERLUDE IN *WERTHER*: in act 1 of Massenet's opera *Werther*, a musical interlude depicts a moonlit garden.

THE BEARD OF THE PATRIARCH OF THE ADRIATIC DESCENDED TOWARD ME LIKE THE CURTAIN OF A WINDOW: possibly a reference to St. Mark, who has links to both Venice (via St. Mark's Basilica) and Aquileia, at the head of the Adriatic, where a Patriarchate was established.

TRANSBAIKAL

NONNI, KERULEN, SELENGA: the names of Transbaikal rivers.

THE COLD WIND OF THE NIGHT

Boie tells us that Gracq here borrows the title of a Leconte de Lisle poem (see *OC* 1, 1227); the phrase also appears in *A Dark Stranger*.

THE MORTE RIVER: the Morte is a river or canal in northwest France; however Gracq plays on a double meaning: "Morte River" is both proper name and "dead river."

THE MYSTICAL LIGHT OF CANDLES ON THE WHITE SHEETS OF THE SNOWY STEPPES SPRANG UP AS FAR AS THE EYE COULD SEE: Michael Riffaterre aligns this sentence with two lines from the Leconte de Lisle poem: "On the plain where the dead are lying down, the snow / Like a shroud stretching out its far distant white covers" (information courtesy of Boie, in *OC* 1, 1227).

WRITTEN IN WATER

The title is in English in the French text: an allusion to Keats's epitaph ("Here lies one whose name was writ in water").

THE ROSS BARRIER

"The Ross Ice Shelf is the largest ice shelf of Antarctica (about the size of France). . . . The ice shelf is named after Sir James Clark Ross, who discovered it on 28 January 1841. It was originally called 'The Barrier' as it prevented sailing further south. In January 1953, the name was changed to 'Ross Ice Shelf'" (Wikipedia, https://en.wikipedia.org/wiki/Ross_Ice_Shelf).

CAPE DISAPPOINTMENT: *Cap de la Dévastation* in French. "It was discovered in 1902 by the Swedish Antarctic Expedition, under Otto Nordenskiöld, and so named by him because he encountered many difficult crevasses in approaching the cape" (Wikipedia, https://en.wikipedia.org/wiki/Cape_Disappointment_(Antarctica)).

JANE RECITED LERMONTOV'S STANZAS FOR ME: see Lermontov's poem "The Sail."

VERGISS MEIN NICHT

Vergissmeinicht, the German name for the myositis—forget-me-not in colloquial English.

FURNISHED SALON

A BIG LIGHTNING-PROOF FARADAY CAGE: a Faraday cage is a container made of conducting material, such as wire mesh or metal plates, that shields what it encloses from external electric fields—hence "lightning-proof."

A CURULE SEAT: in ancient Rome the consul and praetor were entitled to use the *sella curulis*—a kind of folding chair.

AN OPEN PACKET OF SCAFERLATI TOBACCO: Scaferlati tobacco is sliced extremely fine, mainly for the purpose of hand-rolled cigarettes.

A PHOTOGRAPH OF PRESIDENT SADI-CARNOT AT HIS FIRST COM-
MUNION: Sadi-Carnot, president of the Third Republic, was assas-
sinated—stabbed—in 1894 by the Italian anarchist Caserio. The
clearly implied link with the assassination of Caesar is ironic, given
that Caserio is a near anagram.

IN THE SHADOWY REAR OF THE SALON, A TURRETED GOODS WAGON
ON ITS SIDING: Boie comments that "the subject of 'Furnished Sa-
lon' recalls the strange interiors of surrealist pictures and exhibi-
tions—and in its descriptive procedures the collage technique as
evoked by Max Ernst: 'I was struck by the obsession that the pag-
es of an illustrated catalogue exercised over my irritated eyes. . . .
There I found grouped together figural elements that were so dis-
tant that the very absurdity of that assemblage precipitated in me a
sudden intensity of my visionary faculties and gave birth to a hal-
lucinating succession of contradictory images'" (Boie, citing Ernst,
OC 1, 1229). However, the link between Caesar and Sadi-Carnot
suggests that the elements of Gracq's verbal collage aren't quite as
contradictory or dissociated as they might at first seem.

A HIBERNATING MAN

THEN THE RAYS OF THE MOON PROWLED AROUND THE ROOM UNTIL
THE WINDOW PLACED A BIG BLACK CROSS ON THE BED: cf. *A Dark
Stranger*: "Calm moonlight entered through the window from the
area of the park, threw a great black cross on the bed" (*OC* 1, 255).
This statement occurs in the concluding pages of the novel, as the
symbolic omen of a fateful event.

THE DOORS STILL SWUNG ON THEIR HINGES: "les portes restaient battantes"—literally "the doors remained swinging." The value for Gracq of this innocuous-seeming image derives from Breton, who said of *Nadja*, "I wanted it swinging like a door" (cited by Boie, in *OC* 1, 1305). This provided the title for the third chapter of Gracq's book on Breton, *Battant comme une porte*. He commented, "In the wind of those burning pages which, with all his assembled powers, he intends to maintain right to the end *swinging like a door* through which this contagious breath of liberation will long pass" (*André Breton*, *OC* 1, 472, Gracq's emphasis). The link between the open or swinging door and a sense of freedom occurs elsewhere in Gracq, for example in "Gomorrah."

WHITE NIGHTS

"The title constitutes an emblematic citation of Dostoievsky's novel, *White Nights*" (Boie, in *OC* 1, 1230).

LIKE A *CHANSON DE TOILE*: "a medieval song that evokes a young woman seated at her work and talking about he whom she loves" (Larousse, https://www.larousse.fr/dictionnaires/francais/toile/78286#167247). This accounts for the succeeding image of "an artless tapestry frame swept by two blonde tresses. . . ."

IT WAS ALREADY TIME TO GO TO THE ISLANDS: "the islands of the Finnish gulf that were a destination for summer excursions from St. Petersburg" (Boie, in *OC* 1, 1230).

ROBESPIERRE

SOME OF THE LESSER TERRORISTS; SAINT-JUST, JACQUES ROUX, ROBESPIERRE THE YOUNGER: Jacques Roux, defrocked priest, was one of the leaders of the *Enragés*, the ultra-radicals of the French Revolution. He stabbed himself following his arrest in 1793. Robespierre the Younger, brother of Maximilien Robespierre, was executed in 1794, having asked to share his brother's fate.

THE BOUQUETS OF EARS OF CORN, THE HYMNS, THE BREAKFAST IN THE SUN BEFORE THE REVOLUTIONARY CEREMONIES: "Maximilien Robespierre carried a bouquet of ears of corn to the first festival of the Supreme Being, prairial 20 (8 June), 1794" (Boie, in *OC* 1, 1230).

ELECTIVE AFFINITIES

The title refers to Goethe's novel. While there's no apparent relevance to Gracq's text, *Elective Affinities* (the novel) is briefly discussed in *A Dark Stranger*. In *André Breton* Gracq refers to Goethe's borrowing of the chemical term.

THE TRUMPETS OF AIDA

The title is evidently a reference to the triumphal march in the Verdi opera. Gracq was an opera aficionado.

SOME OLD EMPEROR CALLED BULGAROKTONOS: the reference is to the Byzantine Emperor Basil II (958–1025), called Bulgaroktonos, Bulgar Slayer, for his brutal conquest of Bulgaria.

"This is the title of paragraph 16 of the first book of the *Critique of Pure Reason* [Kant], irreverently borrowed by Gracq" (Boie, in *OC* 1, 1231).

THE POET FRANCIS JAMMES AT THE STEERING WHEEL OF HIS STEAM CYLINDER: French poet (1868–1938); Jammes's work primarily addresses rural and religious themes.

I'VE GOT TWO BIG OXEN IN MY STABLE: "J'ai deux grands boeufs dans mon étable." Boie (*OC* 1, 1231) points out that Gracq appropriates here the opening line of a popular nineteenth-century song by Pierre Dupont.

A STATUE OF JOAN OF ARC: Gracq probably refers here to Frémlet's 1874 gilded bronze equestrian statue of Joan of Arc in the Place des Pyramides, Paris.

THE PHOTOGRAPH OF A YOUNG SHRIMPER GIRL: The reference is, I believe, to a photograph of a bronze statue (ca. 1880) by Jean Garnier.

THE ABSORBING IMAGE OF A WOMAN MADE TALLER BY THE STANDARD SHE BEARS: in the Frémlet statue Joan is triumphantly carrying a standard with banner. This implies an ironic comparison with Garnier's much humbler and smaller statue showing a plebian fisher girl carrying her net on a stick over her shoulder.

THE SUSQUEHANNA RIVER

THEIR PRETTY MADAPOLAM CAPS: madapolam is a plain weave cotton or calico cloth.

TROTSKY RECEIVING THE GERMAN PARLIAMENTARIANS IN FRONT OF THE BREST-LITOVSK RAILWAY STATION: the occasion of the 1918 Brest-Litovsk Treaty that extracted revolutionary Russia from World War I: "A direct memory of the event isn't at work in the text, rather its reflection in a colored lithograph; specifically a print in the review *L'Illustration* published at the time, an image that the child's memory has transferred to the poetic universe of the adult" (Boie, in *OC* 1, 1232). This can also be read as a covert allusion to the Molotov-Ribbentrop non-aggression pact of 1939, which caused Gracq to abandon his membership of the Communist Party (see *OC* 2, 1035).

FINE MORNING STROLL

"The title alludes to Arthur Rimbaud's poem 'Bonne pensée du matin' (Pleasant Morning Thought). The complicity arises from an initial thematic similarity, the arousal at daybreak of a big city. But . . . Rimbaud's text has hardly left any other mark on Gracq's prose poem" (Boie, in *OC* 1, 1232).

A FEW CABLES' LENGTH FROM MY ROOM: a cable length is a nautical unit of measure.

THE GREAT GAME

Title ['Le Grand jeu'] of a journal edited by René Daumal with other collaborators. Also the title of a book of poetry by Benjamin Péret.

THE MIDDLE-DISTANCE RUNNER: "The image is tied to personal memories, and in a text in *Lettrines 2* (1974) Gracq will evoke his 'old passion' for middle-distance running" (Boie, in *OC* 1, 1232).

THE ABUNDANT MANCHINEEL TREES OF VENETIAN CHANDELIERS: the manchineel tree is known for its dangerously toxic fruit. The image, as metaphor, occurs elsewhere in Gracq, for example in the preface to his drama, *Le Roi pêcheur* (The Fisher king), which reimagines Wagner's *Parzifal* libretto: "Wagner is a black magician— a manchineel tree with a mortal shadow" (*OC* 1, 331).

THESE TAROTS OF A DUPLICITOUS CARD GAME—TO SEEK FOR WHOM THESE FIGURES, FOR ME ALWAYS SINGULAR, COULD ONLY BE THE SAME ON BOTH SIDES: in one of her notes on *Au Château d'Argol*, Boie cross-references the reversible tarot card of "The Great Game": "image of doubling, the analogy of front and back, the collusion of contraries" (*OC* 1, 1157).

THE BASILICA OF PYTHAGORAS

"The Porta Maggiore Basilica [Rome], a subterranean basilica, was built during the reign of the Roman emperor Nero as a secret place of worship for Pythagoreans. The basilica was built underground because of the Pythagorean emphasis on secrecy ... 12 m (40 ft) below the street level, the underground chamber was discovered accidentally in 1917 during the construction of a railway line." (Wikipedia, https://en.wikipedia.org/wiki/Porta_Maggiore_Basilica). Gracq's text features an old railway station and an underground "initiatory" location.

THE HANGING GARDENS

PARIETARIA JUDAICA: a weed, commonly known as spreading pellitory or pellitory of the wall, a perennial herb growing from the cracks and mortar crevices of brick and stone walls, on building rubble, etc.

THE AMBIGUOUS EMBARKATION

A THOUSAND ST. ELMO FIRES GLOWING ON THE RIGGING: St. Elmo's fire—a phenomenon in which a luminous electrical discharge appears on the mast of a ship during a storm—"carrying the theme of the embarkation, of the journey toward a place of revelation" (Boie, in *OC* 1, 1233).

TRURO

Cathedral city in Cornwall, visited by Gracq in 1933.

THE CONVENT OF THE PANTOCRATOR

Gracq may be referring to the eleventh-century Byzantine monastery of the Pantocrator in Istanbul. Gracq "made no visit to Greece or elsewhere in the western Mediterranean" (Boie, in *OC* 1,1223): if the writer made the visit it was, as with the Ross Barrier and Sertalejo, in his imagination.

THAT TARTAN SETS ITS SAILS: a tartane or tartan was a small ship formerly used as a fishing ship and for coastal trading in the Mediterranean.

ON THE BANK OF THE BEAU BENDÈME

"The title evokes a line of the romance *Ladla* [*sic*] *Rookh* by Thomas Moore, 'Is that bower on the banks of the calm Bendemeer!'" (Boie, in *OC* 1, 1233). Moore's title should, of course, be *Lalla Rookh*.

BLAZONED WITH ROMAN SIGNS AND PHALERAE: phalera (pl. phalerae): (in ancient Greece and Rome) a bright metal disc worn on the chest as an ornament by men.

AN ENTIRE HOGGAR: the Hoggar Mountains are a highland region in the central Sahara in southern Algeria.

THE CLANDESTINE PASSENGER

ITS SAILS BENT TO THE AIR OF ITS THOUSAND MASTS: "bending sails" (*enverguer* in French) is a nautical term for securing sails to their spars. The thousand-masted city setting sail, is, if not a fantastic version of Saint-Nazaire, at least reminiscent of the "ocean-bound" city of "To Galvanize Urbanism."

CORTÈGE

MEN 40–HORSES 8: See the introduction for an explanation of this phrase.

THE *BONNE AUBERGE*

"The name ['The *Bonne Auberge*'—the good hostelry] already figures in André Breton's *Poisson soluble* (Soluble Fish): 'The great lords with jabots of rain, one day I saw them going by on horseback and it was I who received them at the Bonne Auberge' (1924). But ... in the manuscript the text bears the title ... 'Surprise Party at the House of the Augustules'" (Boie, in *OC* 1, 1234). The Augustules title was withdrawn and displaced onto the following text (which in turn displaced its original title). The original title would be more appropriate than "The *Bonne Auberge*," but Gracq's game of musical chairs with titles is a properly surrealist one.

A BEREZINA OF FINE GLASS DEBRIS IS SPREAD OVER THE DESERTED FLOORS: in the winter of 1812, the retreating Napoleonic army crossed the Berezina river in Russia; the crossing was achieved, but at the cost of a massive loss of life.

SURPRISE PARTIES AT THE HOUSE OF THE AUGUSTULES

"Romulus Augustule was the last Roman emperor (475–476) to reign over the western empire. In the manuscript the text is entitled 'The Valley of Josaphat.' The definitive title elicits the mischievousness of the tableau while conserving the reference to the end of a reign which is also the end of a world" (Boie, in *OC* 1, 1234).

THE MONTAGNE SAINTE-GENEVIÈVE: a hill overlooking the Left Bank of the Seine. The churches of Saint Julien and Saint Nicolas are also on the Left Bank. Saint-Julien was the site of a Dadaist excursion organized by Breton in 1921: it was chosen, Breton's biographer remarks, "for its atmosphere of medieval desolation: the abandoned church was falling into ruin . . ." (Mark Polizzotti, *Revolution of the Mind: The Life of André Breton* [London: Bloomsbury, 1995], 152).

The church of Saint Germain L'Auxerois by contrast is on the Right Bank. A class division is implied here; postmen and laundry workers on one side, the archbishop on the other. Historically, the Right Bank is more associated with elite society.

A DENSE HAIL OF BALLS OF LAUNDRY BLUE IS REPORTED AT INTERVALS: *bleu de lessive*—laundry blue, dolly blue, or washing blue. "Laundry blue . . . was largely used for blanching linen until the arrival of chemical detergents. It was sold in the form of blue balls or laundry balls. The shape and the striking color of this commonplace item had already made an impression on André Breton, inspiring this fantasmagorical tableau: 'Elsewhere, probably in a farmyard, a woman juggles several balls of laundry blue that burn in the air like fingernails' (*Poisson soluble*)" (Boie, in *OC* 1, 1234).

THE VALLEY OF JOSAPHAT

"According to biblical prophecy (Joel 4:2), the legendary place where the dead will be assembled for the Last Judgment. . . . The text, written in Caen, no doubt in the course of 1943, commemorates the poet's geographical journey through the diverse regions of Normandy" (Boie, in *OC* 1, 1234).

PARIS AT DAWN

"Written in 1957, the text is clearly marked by the memory of Paris immediately after the war . . . , the awakening of a city that should have been destroyed" (Boie, in *OC* 1, 1235). Boie's comment is cogent; however, the somber mood and imagery of the text also suggests a Paris balanced on a knife-edge between dark fatality and renewal of light. This is Paris as a liminal space, frozen between darkness and light.

"To Galvanize Urbanism" and "Paris at Dawn," along with "The House of the Augustules," are the only imaginative texts by Gracq that specifically identify Paris as their setting.

THOSE LARVAE OF SLOWNESS THAT FLOAT ON THE SHIMMER OF PROPELLER BLADES: Gracq presumably refers here to the "wagon-wheel effect" or "reverse rotation effect"—an optical illusion in which a spoked wheel appears to rotate differently from its true rotation. The image resumes one evoked in *Au Château d'Argol*: ". . . as frightening as the apparent slowness, derisory and so to speak *secondary*, of the blades of a propeller revolving at the upper limit of its speed" (*OC* 1, 61).

THAT ADVENTUROUS HOUR WHEN RASTIGNAC, FROM THE HEIGHTS OF PÈRE-LACHAISE, ANSWERS THE CHALLENGE, IS IN TRUTH A FORBIDDEN HOUR: the reference is to the celebrated final scene of Balzac's *Père Goriot*, when Rastignac, the sole mourner at Goriot's funeral, confronts Paris with a challenge: "À nous deux maintenant"

("It's between us now"). "In a significant inversion Gracq transfers to dawn what was twilight in Balzac" (Boie, in *OC* 1, 1235).

THAT BAUDELAIREAN FRINGE OF THE "PARISIAN DREAM": in Baudelaire's "Rêve parisien" the poet, in his miserable garret, briefly enjoys a dream (implicitly an opium dream) of Paris transformed into a structure of palatial splendor and beauty.

FOR PARIS, AS FOR THE BIBLICAL WATCHMAN, MORNING COMES, AND NIGHT TOO: "Watchman, what is left of the night?" "Morning is coming, but also the night" (Isiah 21:11–12).

MOSES

First published in the journal *Néon*, 3, 1948. "This descent down slow and somber waters, this feminized river" will be taken up again by Gracq in a later account of a boat trip on a river [i.e., *Les eaux étroites* (*The Narrow Waters*)]. No doubt the same memory invests both texts" (Boie, in *OC* 1, 1235). We might also note here the explicit feminization of the Mongolian rivers in "Transbaikal."

ROOF GARDEN

Title given in English in the French text.

THE HIGH PLAINS OF SERTALEJO

Although the setting is clearly South American, specifically Andean, the name "Sertalejo" is invented and the journey is fictional.

FOR JULES MONNEROT: Jules Monnerot (1909–1995) was a sociologist, surrealist, essayist, writer, editor, and colleague of Georges Bataille. Once a fellow schoolboy of Gracq's, they remained close friends. Gracq invoked his writings, particularly *La Poésie moderne et le sacré*, at various points in *André Breton*.

THE ORB OF A STAR: Gracq appears to be using "orb" in the astrological sense; the term is defined as a circle of up to 10° radius around the position of a celestial object.

THE SIESTA IN DUTCH FLANDERS

The French term *La Flandre hollandaise*, which predates the latter-day territorial arrangement, formerly served to distinguish the region from "La Flandre francaise" (now the French département du Nord, or Nord de France). Evidently the term "Dutch Flanders" isn't used in English: we simply refer to Flanders. The French usage should be retained, though; it signals an appropriate territorial ambiguity. Gracq's first experience of the polders was in Holland, and in "The Siesta" he borrows a few phrases from his earlier description of these Dutch polders, transferring them to Belgium (see *Manuscrits de guerre*, 49). Subsequently, the place names he mentions—Baarn, Graauw, Saaftingen—are, respectively, in Holland and the Netherlands. The Amsterdam Rijksmuseum is also mentioned in the text. Having established territorial boundaries at the outset, Gracq goes on to surreptitiously blur them.

FOR MME S. L.: "the dedicatee is Suzanne Lilar, Belgian writer, novelist, dramatist, and essayist. In 1949 she invited Gracq [to

Antwerp] to give his first conference paper outside France ('Surrealism and Contemporary Literature')" (Boie, in *OC* 1, 1236).

THE TERRITORY IS POORLY LINKED TO ZEELAND: i.e., the westernmost and least populous province of the Netherlands.

THE EXPLOSION OF FLORESCENCE THAT FOLLOWS A DELUGE: this sentence quotes an identical sentence in the *Manuscrits de guerre*, 56–57.

LIKE AN INSECT FOLLOWING THE SEAMS OF THE FLOOR: cf. *Récit*, in *Manuscrits de guerre*, 189: "like ants stuck to the seam of the floor."

IN THE AFTERNOON OF THE PRAIRIE: the capitalization here seems to indicate a place name. Cf. the locality of Prairie in Hainaut, Belgium.

THE CONTOURS OF EVERY THOUGHT DISSOLVES INTO THE GREEN MIST: readers of English poetry will be reminded here of a stanza of Andrew Marvell's "The Garden," which anticipates Gracq by some three centuries:

> Meanwhile the mind, from pleasure less,
> Withdraws into its happiness;
> The mind, that ocean where each kind
> Does straight its own resemblance find,
> Yet it creates, transcending these,
> Far other worlds, and other seas;

Annihilating all that's made
To a green thought in a green shade.

Gracq could read English fluently and knew his Shakespeare, but had he read the Marvell poem? We can't know, but it's at least possible; after all one would not have expected a French writer with links to surrealism to be familiar with Moore's *Lalla Rookh*, and "The Garden" is more widely read than that. The preceding reference to an "English lawn" might also suggest a connection with Marvell. Discussing "Siesta" in her "Notice" on *Liberté grande*, Boie explores affinities with sources more surely known to Gracq—German Romanticism, notably Schlegel's *Lucinda*, and Zen Buddhism (Boie, in *OC* 1, 1221–2).

YOU SUCCUMB AT FULL LENGTH, ON THE GRASS: Cf. Marvell: "Ensnared with flowers, I fall on grass."

AN UNANCHORED BOTTLE IMP: *ludion* in French, a classic science experiment that demonstrates the principle of buoyancy.

GOMORRAH

See the introduction for a discussion of this text.

THROUGHOUT THE CINGLAIS THICKETS: "Wooded region to the east of the Orne and south of Caen. In May 1944 its forests and chateaus were occupied by a German armored division. Throughout its entirety the text is held in tension between this dreamy ramble through a holiday landscape and the signs of war that constellate it, on the ground (the tanks, the evacuated manor houses, the refugee camp beds), in the sky (the commotion of the metal flies), even in the seasons (the 'out of joint light' ['la lumière désheurée'])" (Boie, in *OC* 1, 1238).

I ARRIVED AT THE MAY HILLSIDE: "May-sur-Orne, village ten kilometers south of Caen" (Boie, in *OC* 1, 1238).

SHE WAS ALSO STOPPING AT JAUR: "Jaur is the only fictive name in this itinerary so close to reality. It corresponds to the village of Clecy" (Boie, in *OC* 1, 1238).

L'HEURE ALLEMANDE: (italicized in the French text)—the German hour. "Central European hour, two hours in advance of that of Paris and imposed by the occupying powers on all the territories under the Third Reich. This feeling of time liberated from the customary rules, *désheurées* [out of sync], combines with the impression of 'the empty road that flowed limpid and pure . . .'" (Boie, in *OC* 1, 1238). I've retained the French expression. French Wikipedia tells us that "the expression *heure allemande* is generally used as a synonym for German Occupation during the Second World War . . . ever since the 1945 publication of Jean-Louis Bory's novel, *Mon village à l'heure allemande*" (https://fr.wikipedia .org/wiki/Heure_allemande).

AUBRAC

"Aubrac is a small village in the southern Massif Central of France. The name is also applied to the surrounding countryside, which is properly called l'Aubrac in French. . . . Aubrac is a volcanic and granitic plateau that extends over an area of 1,500 km" (Wikipedia, https://en.wikipedia.org/wiki/Aubrac). In a 1978 interview, Gracq, speaking apropos of the Aubrac region, said, "in this landscape you have the feeling that you could go everywhere, you have an impression of astonishing liberties" (*OC* 2, 1205). "Aubrac" was, in 1966, the last written of *Great Liberty*'s texts; the volume in its final revised edition thus encompasses a period of twenty-five years.

IN THE DISTANCE, THE VIADÈNE: "Granite plateau visible to the south of Aubrac" (Boie, in *OC* 1, 1239).

THE PARTRIDGE-GRAY CAUSSE: "the causse du Mende to the southwest of Aubrac" (Boie, in *OC* 1, 1239).

George MacLennan has translated works by Michel de Ghelderode, Marcel Brion, and Marcel Béalu for Wakefield Press.